THE *SKILLS* OF CRICKET

THE *SKILLS* OF CRICKET

KEITH ANDREW
Director of Coaching,
National Cricket Association

THE CROWOOD PRESS

Published by The Crowood Press
Crowood House, Ramsbury
Marlborough, Wiltshire SN8 2HE

Reprinted, 1986
Paperback edition, 1986

British Library Cataloguing in Publication Data

Andrew Keith
    The skills of cricket
    1. Cricket
    I. Title
    796.35'82   GV917

    ISBN 0–946284–30–X

        0–946284–93–8 (PB)

Acknowledgements

*Photographs from Test matches showing players in action are by
Patrick Eagar*

Demonstration photographs by Keith Andrew

Diagrams by John Hawtin

Cover Design by Wendy Bann

Printed in Spain by Graficromo s.a., Cordoba
Typeset by Inforum Ltd, Portsmouth

Contents

Illustrations

The author — Keith Andrew

Keith Andrew joined Northamptonshire County Cricket Club in 1953, and represented England against Australia and the West Indies in 1954 and 1963. During this period he created a number of wicket-keeping records, and in 1962 became one of the youngest professional captains in cricket history, leading his county through five very successful years.

Keith has been involved with cricket for over thirty years as player, administrator and author. He joined the National Cricket Association in 1975, and has been Director of Coaching since 1979.

"Keith Andrew's deep knowledge of cricket is very evident in this book. As N.C.A.'s Director of Coaching, he well represents the breed of men who make cricket the game it is.

"What I really like about Keith's book is that whilst it is very technical, it is not dogmatic and puts forward ideas that a player or coach may adapt to their own requirements. Singular attention is paid to attitudes within the development of individual skill. I am sure that players of all ranges of ability and age will benefit from a careful examination of, not only the varied text, but the magnificent photographs by Patrick Eagar."

David Gower

"This is a real cricketer's book; written with dedication, an intimate knowledge of the game and even a thread of humour, as I would expect from its author.

"Keith Andrew was a fine wicket-keeper and captain. I have spent many happy times with him on cricket's highways and byways.

"I believe this book could well become a classic in its field."

Freddie Brown, C.B.E.
President of the National Cricket Association
Former Captain of England
President of MCC 1972

Introduction

When I first thought of writing this book I believed that it would be a fairly simple matter to draw from previous writings, spice them with a few anecdotes from my own playing experience and maybe flavour the mixture with a few quotes from great players of the past. In fact, it turned out to be entirely different and much more enjoyable when I began with the word "attitudes" as applied to batting. Fortunately, I realised almost immediately that if I was going to have some degree of satisfaction in what I had written the word must be applied not only to batting, but to the game as a whole. Consequently, I had to think again: not to change my ideas technically, but to colour them with the lessons of today as well as yesterday. It became important to discuss the game again, not just with my contemporaries whose knowledge and experience I could count on, but also with today's young players on whose fresh outlook the future of the game depends.

But no matter how well the lessons of all the eras are learned, no matter how marvellous the distilled knowledge of today and yesterday might appear, without a feeling for the true spirit of the game, its enjoyment can never be complete. Let me hope there is something of this between the lines of this book.

In cricket winning is important, or at least playing to win is, but success in cricket is not necessarily winning. Success is to do with the manner in which the game is played, win or lose. In fact, cricket for those who play, or have played, or have wanted to play, is much more than a game. It is a way of life bred on ethics and traditions that have stood the test of time. Cricket is a game of compassion. A youngster need not be born with the physical make-up of an athlete to play well; neither does he or she need to be an academic to appreciate its subtleties. The game caters for all kinds of people, young and old, extrovert and introvert. Attitude, skill and being part of the team, both on and off the field, are what really count. There is a home in cricket for everyone, of ever creed, from any walk of life.

Having said this, albeit so true, it is sometimes hard to appreciate for the young player who cannot get a run or take a wicket. I hope, therefore, that the following pages will be used, not only by coaches to guide their talented protégés, but also by teachers and parents to help those who may not be quite so talented, but who have equal potential for improvement and enjoyment of the game. Most of all, I hope that keen cricketers, young and old, will themselves study aspects of their own part in the game and practise hard to improve their performance, so that it will be recognised where it counts – out there in the middle.

Cricketers everywhere, and particularly young cricketers, are great mimics. Knowing this, I have based my technical comments on a series of excellent photographs of the world's finest players in action. I emphasise "in action" not to criticise the value of posed photographs or drawings, in themselves so necessary for good instruction, but simply to show that the techniques described are based upon actual play at the highest level. Of course, photographs and drawings alone are not enough either, if more than lip service is to be paid to the task of realising a positive improvement in your performance. You need to study them in conjunction with the related text and diagrams. I should also like to stress the importance of the Laws of Cricket. Many are the batsmen and bowlers who have failed to progress, simply because they have not had a proper knowledge of even one or two of them, particularly the LBW and No Ball Laws. How many games must have been won or lost, simply because an enterprising captain has known the Laws and used that knowledge? If nothing else, a recapitulation will perhaps emphasise the difficulty of the umpire's job and persuade the player that forgivable mistakes can be made.

Some of the problems of cricket, like its blessings, are in its traditions. In the not too distant past organised practice was almost frowned upon, at least in terms of practising with an objective. Even the players that had the opportunity of practising in nets and on good pitches more often than not unconsciously practised their faults, rather than trying to cure them. Physical fitness as a subject was not considered as an integral part of the game. However, as enthusiasm for the proper coaching of the game has increased and as science has been harnessed for use in sport, so has the opportunity been created for greater enterprise and enjoyment at all levels of the game.

Times have changed. Whether for the better remains to be seen. Meanwhile, I have tried to ensure that the great skills that have made cricket the game it is can be more easily appreciated by an increasingly eager following of enthusiasts who want to play with some success and enjoy the game in the delightful environment that is so much its own.

Keith Andrew

1 Length and Direction

Before becoming too involved in analysing the various cricket skills, it is important to understand certain concepts of the game that concern both batsman and bowler. Only through this knowledge will you be able to improve your technique on sound principles. Because of the abstract and comparatively complex nature of some of these concepts, over the years they have acquired a mystique that cricketers themselves delight in, when projecting their game to the outsider. Of course, the arguments that are brought forth are part of cricket's attraction, as in the end we all like to interpret the game in our own way. Nevertheless, to gloss over the mysteries of length, for example, would, I feel, be like starting to climb a mountain without a rope, or maybe learning to drive a car using only one gear, or some similar analogy.

Length

I read and hear much formal discourse on cricket, but I have never yet known the subject of length be fully discussed outside the dressing-room. The word "length" in cricket refers to the point at which the ball pitches in relation to the batsman when in his normal stance at the wicket. Fully understanding the meaning of a "good length" in all the circumstances you might encounter in a match is one of cricket's most difficult problems, applying equally, but for different reasons, to batsmen and bowlers.

A good length may be described as that length of delivery that causes the batsman most hesitation as to whether to play back or forward. To bowl a good length at will is the objective of every bowler. Many cricketers learn the meaning of a good length through hard experience. Others, who are few and far between, are born with the gift of ball sense that enables them to recognise a good length instinctively. Because of differences in physical make-up, speed of reaction and technical ability, what may be a good length to one batsman need not be to another. Similarly, a good length bowled by a slow bowler is different from that bowled by a quicker bowler if it is to achieve the same reaction from the batsman in terms of doubt as to whether to play back or forward. The prevailing atmospheric conditions, the state of the playing surface and even the condition of the ball, whether it be old or new, are important influences on what is a good length for a particular delivery. For example, when the ball is new and the atmosphere is heavy and conducive to the ball swinging, a good length is slightly nearer the batsman than it would otherwise be. On slower playing surfaces (pitches), a good length is again nearer to the batsman than it would be on a quicker surface.

Bounce

I nearly left it at that, but one of my colleagues, Bob Carter, one time Worcestershire fast bowler, who kindly checked the manuscript for technical errors, thought it might be worthwhile for me to

The Skills of Cricket

make some comment on "bounce". On reflection, I very much agree with him, although in advance, let me suggest that inexperienced cricketers do not get too involved in this subject.

To start, one might say that bounce is to do with the speed of the playing surface – a fast or a slow pitch, or wicket as it is often referred to. It is true that generally the faster the playing surface, the higher the bounce. This is not always the case, however, as bad or wet surfaces sometimes produce excessive bounce without them being particularly fast. Again, the ball itself bounces differently as it becomes older. Also, providing they deliver the ball with a high action, tall bowlers obviously achieve more bounce than those not so tall. Bounce can have many interpretations, but I am looking at it in the context of "length" and its relationship with batting, or more specifically, its effect on the batsman's decision to play forward or back. There is no doubt that the good batsman in planning his innings has, if possible, taken the likely variations that influence bounce into consideration. He will, knowing his own style of play, have some idea of how he will cope with high or low bounce. Invariably, the most displeasing pitch on which a batsman can play is one on which bounce is variable from a constant length.

So to the main reason for this discourse; back or forward – forward or back? When and how? Good batsmen are instinctive in their reactions, but a good batsman is a prepared batsman. *If anticipated bounce is low, look to play forward – back, if the bounce is likely to be high*. But what is high and low? High bounce may be interpreted by a batsman as that bounce of delivery that hits the bat splice or higher when playing normally forward to a good length ball. Low bounce may be interpreted as that bounce of delivery that would hit the batsman below knee height when playing normally back. Depending upon anticipated bounce and the style of batsman he is bowling to, a good length varies for each type of bowler. In general, the higher the bounce, the nearer the batsman the attacking bowler will pitch the ball, looking to bring him forward and commit him to a stroke. If the batsman is known as a committed forward player in any

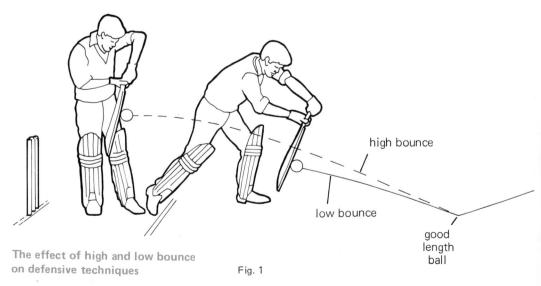

high bounce

low bounce

good
length
ball

The effect of high and low bounce
on defensive techniques   Fig. 1

4

case, the bowler will be more effective shortening his length a little and vice versa for the committed back player.

Looking back at this discourse, I become acutely aware of "disturbing" a complex subject, but I hope readers will find ensuing discussions as stimulating as Bob and I did.

Recognised Names for Length of Delivery

GOOD LENGTH

As described previously, this is the length bowlers must be looking to pitch nearly every ball. Occasionally a bowler may deliberately try to bowl a yorker or a bouncer in an effort to surprise and therefore dismiss a batsman. An appreciation of a good length can be acquired to some degree by the recognition of what is *not* a good length. The following descriptions of various length deliveries will emphasise this point.

LONG HOP

A delivery that pitches approximately half-way down the pitch, slow enough for the batsman to consider it a gift. Can be hit hard anywhere in front of the wicket, but generally is pulled on the leg-side.

SHORT BALL

Short bowling is bad bowling. Depending upon direction the batsman can play any one of the attacking back strokes to a short delivery on a good surface. Even on a bad pitch the short ball can cost runs.

SHORT OF A LENGTH

Pitching much nearer to the batsman than the long hop, or short ball, this delivery is, as its name implies, short of a good length. A defensive delivery on a good pitch, it can be a useful wicket-taker on a difficult pitch (when the ball is lifting or keeping low) for the faster bowlers.

HALF VOLLEY

Pitching beyond a good length, this is the delivery that every batsman should be looking to hit hard just after it pitches – and yet when the ball is swinging and the batsman is not well set, it can be a wicket-taker through catches behind the wicket.

YORKER

Pitching approximately at the batsman's feet, the yorker is a very effective wicket-taker (bowled) if delivered with a little extra pace. A surprise delivery that can easily become a full toss or half volley.

FULL TOSS

Like the long hop, this delivery is looked upon by batsmen as a gift. Not pitching at all, the height at which the ball reaches the batsman can determine the stroke.

BOUNCER

Much has been said and written about the bouncer. It pitches generally in a similar area to the long hop, but is delivered at an extremely fast pace. The ball pitches and lifts towards the batsman's chest and head.

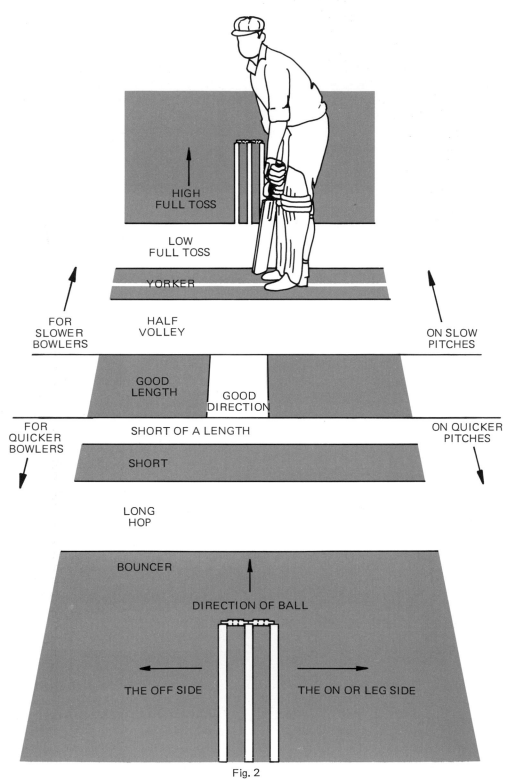

Fig. 2

BEAMER

A head-high full toss. Under no circumstances should any bowler attempt to bowl this delivery, as it can be dangerous to the batsman.

SUMMARY

The length of a delivery determines the stroke a batsman will attempt. If the correct stroke is played for the length bowled, a batsman will be likely to score and in most circumstances will certainly retain his wicket. If a batsman misjudges length and plays the incorrect stroke, it is likely that he will be dismissed.

In all the batting skills described in Chapter 2, care has been taken to ensure that the type of delivery for each stroke is clearly stated. Hence the importance of these notes.

Direction

Allied to good length and equally important is good direction. The ball should be directed either on or just outside the off-stump in most circumstances.

In the same way that length is perhaps not considered deeply enough in cricket, neither is direction. There really is so much to consider, that understandably young players want to get on with bowling, hitting and catching the ball. However, I think it is worthwhile looking at this aspect of bowling in more depth now, rather than later.

The basic requirement of good direction is to pitch the ball on a good length some-where between the middle and just outside the off-stump, with the primary object of making the batsman play at the ball. This makes sense when considering that the

more skilled batsmen are more often than not dismissed early in their innings through catches behind the wicket. However, the batsman will only *have* to play at the ball if he thinks that by not doing so, the ball may hit the wicket.

On good pitches, with little movement of the ball in the air or off the pitch, it is fair to assume that the ball will continue its line of initial direction before and after pitching. In which case, should the bowler deliver the ball from wide on the bowling crease, it is more likely to easily miss the wicket than if the delivery had been from close to the stumps, i.e. bad, rather than good direction (*Fig 3a*). When conditions allow the ball to move considerably in the air (swing bowling) or off the pitch (spin bowling), the reverse situation applies in that to achieve good direction, that is *make* the batsman play at the ball, it can be necessary for the bowler to deliver the ball from wide rather than from close to the stumps (*Fig 3b*). A little study will soon confirm that the bowler's delivery position at the crease will depend upon the anticipated movement of the ball, either off the pitch or through the air. Whilst variation will always be a key-word in good bowling, in most instances, and certainly when bowling at the better batsmen, the bowler will be looking to find a thin edge of the bat through the compromise of delivery position and anticipated movement of the ball.

A bowler is said to be bowling over the wicket if his bowling arm is on the side nearest the stumps on delivery. He is bowling round the wicket when his body comes between the stumps and his bowling arm on delivery. Generally, bowlers only bowl round the wicket when there is considerable movement of the ball in towards the batsman (i.e. off-spinners; right-arm inswing bowlers). The exception to this generalisation is the slow left-arm

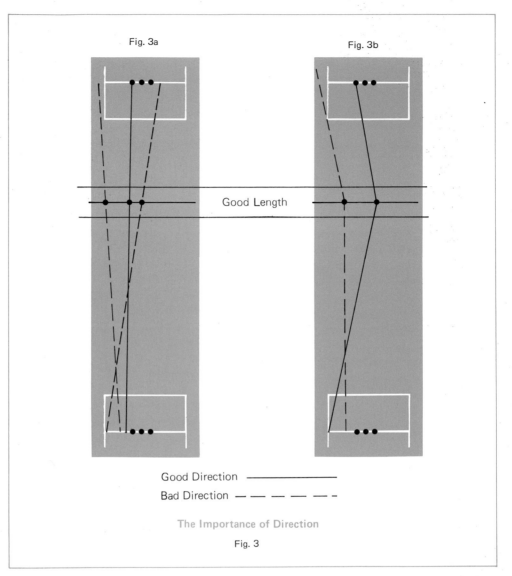

Fig. 3a

Fig. 3b

Good Length

Good Direction ————————

Bad Direction — — — — — —

The Importance of Direction

Fig. 3

finger-spin bowler who always tends to bowl round the wicket. I must confess I cannot see the reason for this on good pitches and feel that the slow left-armer may well benefit from bowling over the wicket in such circumstances. It is certainly worth experiment. Summarising, it may be said that it is good practice to bowl mainly from close to the stumps on whichever side of the wicket you are bowling, although the batsman should never be able to entirely predict the source of good direction.

2 Batting

Attitudes

I am sure that every batsman, young or old, talented or otherwise, must dream at some time of playing the ultimate innings, despatching the greatest bowlers to all parts of the ground with a glittering display of strokes. In reality such innings rarely occur, but there is no reason why any batsman should not improve by adopting a more realistic approach to the game. How many batsmen, week in and week out, play beautifully until reaching double figures? Then, for some reason or another, they virtually change character and attempt to play strokes that are simply not on. In astonishing self-deceit, they resort to blaming the pitch, the umpire, the light, the bat, or even the "night before" for their lack of success. Maybe occasionally the bowler gets credit, but seldom does the batsman admit that he just cannot play the stroke that leads to his downfall. Perhaps it is likely that during a hard week's work, a glimpse of some great batsman on television has caused a "rush of blood" and the desire to smash the ball into another world – and why not indeed. At a guess though, I think most of those who fall early in their innings would love another chance and next time they would play the stroke to perfection. That is, of course, after having practised some of the techniques of batting described in the following pages!

First things first and whilst you do not have to become an Olympic athlete, reasonable physical fitness is a must for any batsman worth his salt. The chapter on Fitness presents a simple range of training that should suit most requirements.

A problem confronting many cricketers is that they find themselves guided into styles of play and sections of the game to which they are not necessarily suited, either physically or mentally. Whenever you are learning a new technique, it should only be practised in the knowledge that it is achievable. Always assess your own capabilities. Am I strong, tall, short; am I a fast runner or do I rival the local cart-horse? To support the question, look at others or cast your mind back to the great batsmen of the past. Think of the strengths exhibited by the best batsmen that you know personally. I will wager that you find the taller chaps are good drivers, using the top hand to present the most vertical of bats, and that the shorter fellows tend to be stronger with the bottom hand and have made their names by cutting and pulling, only driving occasionally through very quick footwork. Why not study and practise the strokes that are most likely to suit you? Are you mainly a front foot player or a back foot player? For some reason or other, it has always been fashionable for English batsmen to cultivate the drive, whilst overseas batsmen have been more varied in their approach. The vertical, or what is termed the straight bat, is the hallmark of English batsmanship at its best. Yet those great players with the unforgettable names, Hobbs, Sutcliffe, Hammond, Hutton, Washbrook, Compton, May, Cowdrey, Graveney, Barrington, Dexter and more recently, Boycott, were all masters of the back defence in addition to the drive. Currently we see this point confirmed by great batsmen like Greg

The Skills of Cricket

Chappell of Australia, Viv Richards of the West Indies, Zaheer Abbas of Pakistan, and our own David Gower. Yes, there is not a batsman alive who would not improve his game a lot if he improved his back foot play by a little. Recognise that a straight bat can be presented to the ball horizontally as well as vertically and also take note that those who play strokes off the back foot have much more of the field to aim at than those who play strokes off the front foot. These points are made to give food for thought, for when all is said and done, the truly elegant stroke in cricket is the cover drive played by a master.

Perhaps the biggest "getting out" stroke in cricket is the on-drive. Very few batsmen can play it well and I have even discouraged players from trying to play the stroke. Generally they play it badly, and the fault seems to stay with them forever. This may be the stroke that limits your success.

Batsmen are well advised to discuss aspects of batsmanship between themselves and also with their coaches. Sometimes a reduced range of strokes will give a batsman the encouragement to play more to his strengths. By concentrating on playing fewer strokes, not only does he learn to play them better, but almost certainly his confidence will increase and his whole attitude will become more positive. I have seen it happen more than once and I have also heard it said somewhere that the one place batsmen cannot get runs is in the dressing-room! In adopting a positive attitude, a player's role in the team seems to become more effective, especially on the occasions when wickets have to be sacrificed in the quest for quick runs.

Different batsmen naturally have different ways of coping with the first ball they receive and, of course, this in itself depends upon position in the batting order and the state of the game at the time. Many leading batsmen I know take a shorter grip on the bat (drop their bottom hand) when they first go to the wicket. Others concentrate on really watching the ball and not committing themselves to a too early movement of the head. Probably the best tip I can give any batsman when waiting to receive any ball is instead of thinking "how can I stop this ball hitting my wicket?", make a positive effort to say to yourself "how can I score off this ball?". You will be surprised at yourself once you have caught the habit.

There is no doubt about the fact that the "thinking" cricketer is the one to watch and can very often gain a place in the team in front of the more gifted player who may be a "non-thinker". For example, non-thinking batsmen will play the most magnificent strokes always in the same direction and with the same strength. Similarly, they will defend without the thought of stealing a run. Good opposing captains quickly realise the situation and brief their fielders accordingly. The result is that in frustration the batsman in question gets himself out, trying to play a shot he is not capable of playing. A thinking batsman will always assess the position and ability of the opposing fielders, placing his strokes accordingly.

This also helps in the always difficult art of running between wickets. Everyone on the field should know that on slow pitches the ball tends to go square rather than fine off the bat. On very slow pitches firm-footed driving can be a waste of time and wickets. Without being too committed, batsmen should discuss with their captain what might be a good score under the conditions and in the time available. There are occasions when even the most orthodox batsmen must throw caution to the wind and take calculated risks to hit the ball into vacant parts of the field, or even out of it! A team's innings cannot be planned totally beforehand, but if every batsman plays his part unselfishly, tactics can be planned as the innings progresses. It has been said that bowlers win matches. I am not so sure that a good team batting effort does not do just as well as any bowling combination.

As we move on to study the details of the many skills in batting, it is worth repeating that batsmen get themselves out as much by playing the right shot to the wrong ball as playing the wrong shot to the right ball. Think about it! Whichever, there is no doubt that all the practice in the world is no good unless having perfected a stroke, you position yourself to give an identity to the delivery of the ball, whether it be a good length or a half volley or long hop etc. To exaggerate, it is no use trying to play the perfect square-cut to an inswinging half volley!

The Basics of Batting

To simplify descriptions, it is assumed, unless otherwise stated, that a right-handed batsman is at the wicket.

When a batsman is out of form and cannot get a run, even in the best of conditions, it is unlikely that the critics will focus their attention on the three factors in batsmanship that may well be the cause of the trouble. That is, the Grip, the Stance, or the Backlift. Yet if a batsman scores a lot of runs, but slowly, the pundits can be expected to put the entire blame on his "peculiar" grip, not his unwillingness to force the pace. A batsman not making runs for two or three innings, obviously because of a bad pitch, may easily find the stance from which he made hundreds only weeks before the subject of a heated debate. Credit or criticism does not always go where it is due, with the result that very often the fundamentals of good batsmanship are

ignored until it is too late. I cannot over-emphasise the importance of continuously checking these three foundations of sound technique.

GRIP *(Figs 4 and 5)*

1. Both hands should be close together, the top hand particularly gripping the handle very firmly. In normal circumstances approximately one inch of bat handle will protrude.

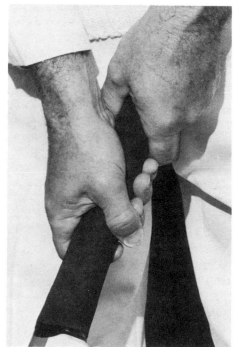

Fig 4   The grip: side view.

2. The "vees" formed by thumbs and first fingers should be in line and pointing somewhere between the splice and the outside edge of the bat. The alignment of the "vees" is of the utmost importance. A driver of the ball with a full follow-through will be setting his "vees" as near to the outside edge as his wrist will comfortably allow when playing fully forward

defensively. A "check" driver and the defensively inclined batsman will be setting his "vees" more in line with the splice. A compromise is recommended and this should give a batsman the best of both worlds. The important thing is to know what your method is and check it regularly.

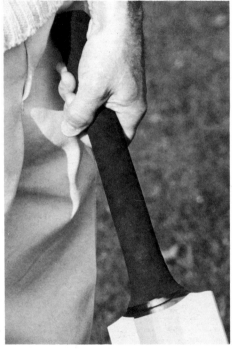

Fig 5   The grip: top hand.

STANCE *(Figs 6 and 7)*

No matter what a batsman's aspirations; no matter what his style, without the sound base of a good stance, his performance is very likely to be limited.

1. The feet are positioned on either side of the batting crease approximately a bat's width apart. Too narrow a stance loses balance, too wide a stance reduces mobility. Weight should be evenly distributed on both feet, never entirely on the heels. The back foot should be parallel to the crease, the front foot either parallel or slightly open (pointing to cover point).

2. The knees are slightly flexed to encourage quick movement of the feet when necessary. Hips are slightly more open than the shoulders.

3. The back of the top hand will generally face between mid-off and cover, depending upon the batsman's preference for angling the bat in his stance. The side of the top hand rests very lightly against the thigh.

4. Line the shoulders up to point straight down the pitch when a right-arm bowler is bowling over the wicket. If the bowler should change his delivery position, the batsman should change his shoulder line accordingly.

5. The head should be turned fully towards the bowler, with the eyes as level as possible.

6. Do not crouch. Stand as "tall" as possible and always feel comfortable in your stance.

Neither the head nor the feet should move until the ball has been properly sighted and the length judged. Nature being what it is, the ideal positions noted are not always attainable by all batsmen and allowances can be made. For example, those who cannot remain sideways with their eyes level, may open their stance slightly. That is, allow the shoulder to point more towards mid-on. When playing at the ball on or outside the off-stump however, a pronounced shoulder turn will be needed to achieve the correct position to strike the ball. Others, rather than open their stance, will lift their bat off the ground in the stance position to retain the classic body position.

Batsmen who have succeeded with this open stance are Ken Barrington of England and one of the most prolific run scorers of all time, the great Bill Ponsford of Australia. More recently, Peter Willey of Northamptonshire and England has scored centuries against West Indian fast bowling

Fig 6   Sir Garfield Sobers – the stance of
           aggression. The hint of a crouch, but a
           magnificent head position.

Fig 7 *Allan Lamb gives the feeling of balance and being ready for action, as does Bob Taylor behind the wicket.*

from an open stance, and again from the photographs of the distant past, George Gunn, Maurice Leyland and even Sir Jack Hobbs were not exactly orthodox. The bat lifters include Dr. W. G. Grace himself and in recent years, Tony Greig. In fact, the really tall batsmen seem to have no choice, if they are not to crouch. Of current players, Graham Gooch is the best example of a bat lifter.

When a batsman goes to the wicket, prior to him receiving the first ball, he asks the umpire to give him a guard. That is, by holding the bat vertically in front of the wicket, the toe of the bat resting on the crease, he is able to mark (scratch) the batting crease in such a way that he knows exactly where he stands in relation to the wicket when in the stance position.

BACKLIFT *(Fig 8)*

Without a well-grooved and technically sound backlift, no batsman can hope to achieve any consistency in striking the ball.

1. Start the backlift early before any other movement, so that the actual stroke is not rushed.
2. Let the top hand take control.
3. Extend the front arm backwards to give a wide sweep with a minimum flex of the elbow.
4. Let the wrists cock naturally to open the bat face.
5. Allow the front forearm to be at least parallel to the ground with the wrist finishing higher than the elbow.
6. Let the shoulder be "pulled" under the chin, the eyes closely watching the bowler's hand.
7. Try to pick the bat up in a line between wicket and wicket. Some very successful batsmen, including Sir Donald Bradman, have picked the bat up towards first and even second slip, but photographs tell us that they "loop" at the top to give a straight downswing towards the ball and through the intended line of stroke.
8. Allow the elbows to clear the body for the high backlift.
9. Keep the head still.

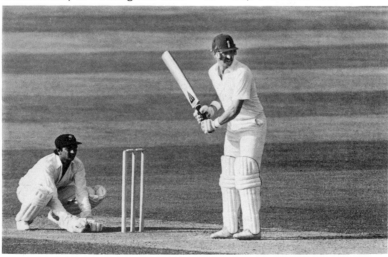

Fig 8   Graham Gooch — the beginning of a classical backlift. Note that there has been no movement of either head or feet.

BACK STROKES *(Fig 10)*

Important – in all back strokes the back foot should remain parallel to the crease throughout its initial movement.

I have heard it said that batsmen should learn to play the attacking strokes before they learn to defend. The theory is that if they learn to defend first, they will become restricted and never ever be able to hit the ball hard. I cannot agree with this and I see no reason why attack and defence should not be learned and practised together. One thing is certain; if a batsman does not have a sound defence, he will not remain at the wicket long enough to play many attacking strokes. With this in mind, I have commenced this section of batting with the defensive back stroke.

Fig 9   *Graham Gooch plays back in the West Indies. Back foot parallel to crease and high front elbow keeps him in line as the ball slants in.*

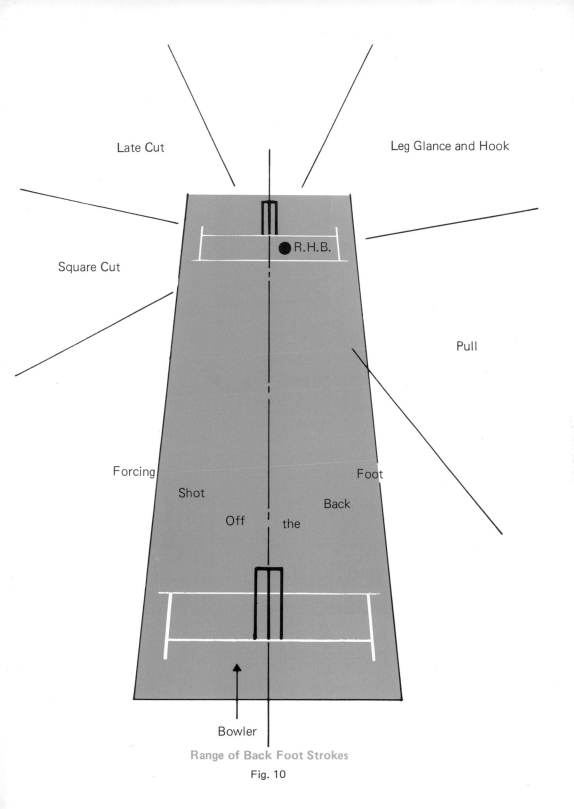

Late Cut

Leg Glance and Hook

Square Cut

Pull

R.H.B.

Forcing

Foot

Shot

Back

Off   the

Bowler

Range of Back Foot Strokes

Fig. 10

17

Fig 11   *Allan Lamb demonstrates all the essential*
points in sound defence.

18

Defensive Back Stroke
(Figs 9 and 11)

Played to:

1. A short of a length delivery pitched on the wickets, or just outside the off-stump.

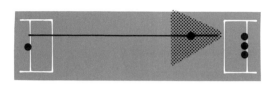

2. A good length delivery pitched on the wickets or just outside the off-stump, depending upon the technique of the batsman concerned and the prevailing conditions.

It is fair to say that in defence, batsmen tend to play back to the faster bowlers and forward to the slower bowlers.

COMMENT

Batsmen are dismissed far more often when trying to play this stroke than the forward defensive. This results in a general encouragement to play forward, rather than learning to play back correctly. Hence the saying "if in doubt, push out". Whilst the back defensive stroke is the more difficult stroke to learn, it is worth persevering with for the dividends it will pay later.

CHECKPOINTS

1. From a sound stance and backlift, the front shoulder moves just inside the line of the ball, the head leading the balance of the body forward.
2. At the same time, the back foot is taken back parallel with the crease and as far as possible, commensurate with the speed of the ball.
3. The weight is almost entirely on the ball of the back foot, the knee being slightly flexed. The front foot acts only as a balance.
4. The top hand in firm control brings the bat face down the line of the ball, with the front elbow high and bent to an approximate right angle.
5. A light thumb and forefinger grip by the bottom hand, with the elbow tucked in to the side, keeps the bat vertical.
6. There is no follow-through, the bat handle being angled forward to keep the ball down.
7. Throughout the stroke, the head remains down behind the ball, the eyes looking over or round the bat handle.

NOTE

The very awkward good length ball pitching on or just outside the leg-stump can be more easily dealt with by allowing the leading shoulder to dip slightly towards the ball. This causes the hips to turn slightly, clearing a path for a straight downswing of the bat.

The Skills of Cricket

ATTACKING BACK STROKES

Forcing Shot *(Fig 12)*

Played to:

1. A short of a length delivery pitching just outside the line of wicket.

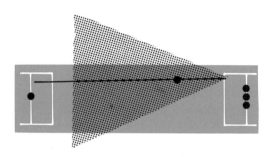

2. A long hop that keeps low, or a low full toss.

NOTE

Do not play this stroke on a bad pitch or against the swinging or turning ball, unless it is very short.

COMMENT

This stroke is becoming one of the most important in the game for a number of reasons:

1. Along with the drive it covers the widest scoring area, ranging from cover to wide mid-on.
2. When played with a "check finish", it is the safest of all the attacking strokes, becoming increasingly popular amongst top-class batsmen as a "bread and butter" stroke that can be played with control off the nagging short of a length delivery.
3. When played with a full follow-through, it is again the safest of the really hard hit strokes.

CHECKPOINTS

1. Follow the basic movements of the back defensive stroke, but with different intention.
2. Make maximum use of your height. Standing with your weight mainly on the ball of your back foot, hit from a firm base.
3. Hitting the ball hard, the rear shoulder drives under the chin, taking the hands high in the full follow-through, as shown in the photograph.

The Check Finish

This technique requires the wrists to remain firm at impact, rather than breaking them to give a full follow-through. The top elbow remains bent to an approximate right angle throughout the stroke, giving support to the check action, which continues until the stroke is complete.

Whilst the check finish enables some young players to force the ball more easily and correctly on both sides of the wicket, it is important for them also to learn to play the forcing shot with the full follow-through. This applies particularly when given the opportunity to hit a rank bad ball. Obviously with a full follow-through the ball can be hit much harder, if not with quite the same control.

Fig 12   *Clive Lloyd plays a typical West Indian forcing shot with the full follow-through.*

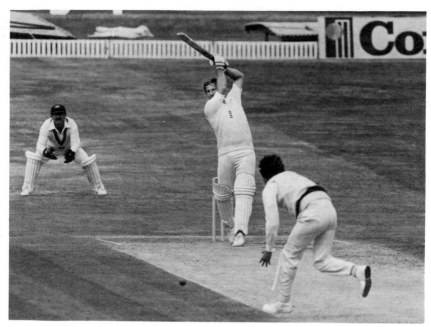

Fig 13   Ian Botham shows that the check finish does not restrict his aggression!

Pull Stroke (Hit to Leg)
(Fig 14)

Played to:

1. A long hop (missing the wicket).

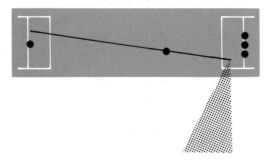

2. A short delivery pitched outside the leg-stump that bounces normally, but never more than chest height.

COMMENT

Move quickly into position and take extra care to watch the ball onto the bat.

CHECKPOINTS

1. Begin this stroke with the basic backlift and movements for the back defensive stroke.

2. As the back foot pivots, the body opens and the ball is hit at full arm stretch as the weight transfers to the other foot (left for right-handed batsmen).

3. When pulling the short delivery of such a pace that complete weight transfer is not possible, take care not to fall away from the ball too early. This can easily produce a half-hit stroke off the top edge of the bat.

4. The balance should be forward towards the pitch of the ball as much as possible throughout this stroke.

5. Take care to direct the stroke in front of square-leg by getting the head right behind the line of the ball, and hit the ball down.

Fig 14   *Viv Richards pulls a short delivery for a
certain four. To reach this position a
batsman needs lightening reflexes.*

Fig 15   Peter Willey hooks with poise and control.

24

The Hook Stroke *(Fig 15)*

Played to a fast, very short, rising delivery pitched on the stumps or just outside the leg-stump, reaching the batsman above chest height.

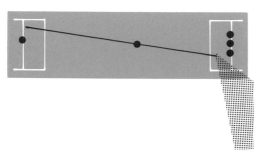

COMMENT

This stroke should only be attempted by experienced and very capable batsmen. If played well, it has a high tactical value, but even so should only be used with discretion. Be prepared to "duck" if you are not in the right position to play the stroke and above all, do not take your eyes off the ball.

CHECKPOINTS

1. Follow the same mechanics for this stroke as for the pull, taking care in this case to position your head outside (off-side) the line of the ball, so that if missed, it will go over the left shoulder (right-handed batsman).
2. Quick footwork will enable you to direct the ball square or fine. Concentrate on this aspect of the stroke. It is possible to hook a ball higher, but trying to hit the high ball down is not recommended. In most instances, it is simply not possible.

Square-cut *(Fig 16)*

Played to:

1. A wide short delivery outside the off-stump.

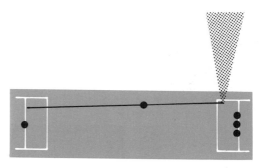

2. A wide fast long hop outside the off-stump that bounces to at least stump height.

COMMENT

An essential stroke for the free-scoring batsman and a prolific run-getter for its best exponents. Take care not to "make room" for this stroke by backing away from the line of the ball.

CHECKPOINTS

1. From a sound stance and backlift, the front shoulder and head turn just inside the line of the ball.
2. The weight is taken completely on the back foot, which automatically moves across and points approximately in the direction of the intended stroke (ideally between point and cover point).
3. A flexible back knee allows the bat to be presented to the ball in as horizontal a plane as possible.
4. From a high backlift, the ball is hit easily at

Fig 16   Greg Chappell's square-cut shows all the
quality of the stroke.

full arm stretch. The bottom hand controls the stroke and the wrists roll enough to direct the ball and keep it down.

5. The back shoulder drives under the chin, allowing a long follow-through of the arms.

The Late-cut *(Fig 17)*

Played to:

1. A short of a length delivery wide of the off-stump.

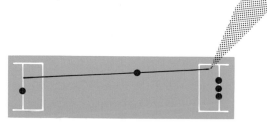

2. This stroke is played to a ball that is not so wide as that to which the square-cut is played.

COMMENT

An elegant old-fashioned stroke now coming back into its own, as limited-over cricket results in vacant slip positions. A stroke to play when your eye is in; not before.

CHECKPOINTS

Similar to the square-cut, but hit closer to the body and not at full arm stretch. The stroke is played with the wrists and a late hit down, wide of the slips.

Fig 17   Geoff Boycott late-cuts with style.

The Leg-glance (Back Foot) *(Fig 18)*

Played to:

1. A short of a length delivery either pitching leg-stump or just outside, but going down the leg-side.

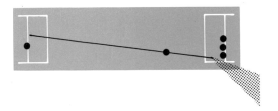

2. A good length delivery pitching leg-stump or just outside, going down the leg-side.

COMMENT

Take care not to play this stroke outside the body — it may result in a catch to the wicket-keeper. Neither should the stroke be played to a ball that would hit the wicket.

CHECKPOINTS

Almost up to the point of contact play this stroke exactly as the back defensive stroke on the leg-stump. Keep the bat handle forward to keep the ball down, bringing the bottom hand into the stroke as late as possible. Using the wrists, angle the bat and place the ball between square and fine-leg, taking care not to try to hit the ball too fine. This stroke is most effective on fast pitches.

Fig 18   Allan Lamb demonstrates the leg-glance, turning his wrists over at impact to direct the ball wide of the fielders.

THE FORWARD STROKES *(Fig 19)*

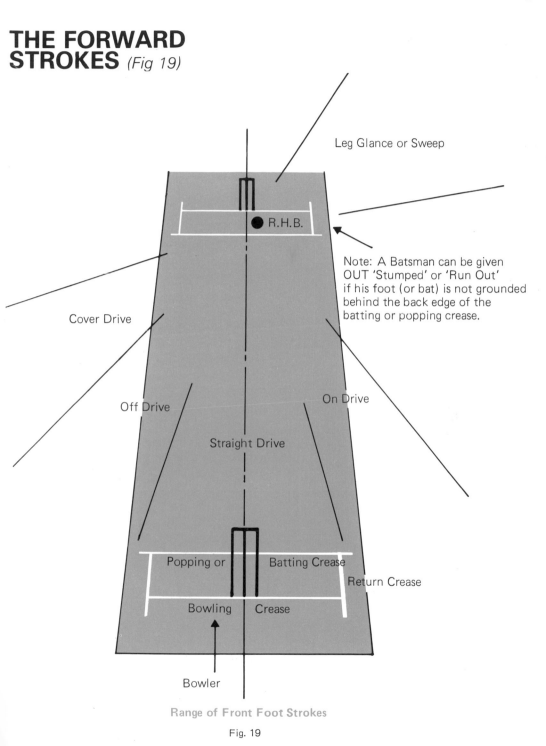

Leg Glance or Sweep

● R.H.B.

Note: A Batsman can be given OUT 'Stumped' or 'Run Out' if his foot (or bat) is not grounded behind the back edge of the batting or popping crease.

Cover Drive

Off Drive

On Drive

Straight Drive

Popping or   Batting Crease

Return Crease

Bowling   Crease

Bowler

Range of Front Foot Strokes

Fig. 19

29

The Skills of Cricket

Important – let the front shoulder and head lead all forward strokes.

If a vote was taken amongst batsmen, I am sure the front foot drives would come out on top as being the most exhilarating strokes in cricket. At the same time, the mishit drive is perhaps the stroke that gives the bowler his best return, whether the catch be at deep mid-off or in the slips. It is important therefore, to recognise the good length delivery that necessitates a more circumspect forward defensive stroke, which, whilst it is the easier of the two defensive strokes to play, still needs the background of a sound technique.

FORWARD DEFENSIVE STROKES
(Fig 20)

The most commonly used stroke in English cricket, probably developed to the state it is because of the old adage "if in doubt, push out". If not, it is certainly a product of the "not getting out" philosophy. Of course, this is an essential and primary stroke in the repertoire of any batsman.

Played to:

A good length ball pitching on the wickets or just outside the off-stump.

COMMENT

The main problem in playing the forward defensive stroke is making the forward movement of the front foot too early, before picking up the line and judging the length of the ball.

CHECKPOINTS

1. From a sound stance and backlift, lead with the front shoulder and head just inside the line of the ball.
2. The hips will follow the shoulder, as will the front leg and foot.
3. The front foot moves as far as comfortably possible towards and just inside the line of the ball.
4. The front knee bends just beyond the vertical, keeping the ball down if it is edged on to the front pad. It also closes the gap between bat and pad.
5. The weight is almost entirely on the front foot. The back leg is fully extended and grounded on the inside of the foot.
6. There is no follow-through, as the bat handle is angled forward by a very firm top hand grip and a light thumb and forefinger bottom hand grip.
7. The front elbow is high and at an approximate right angle, keeping the bat face vertical and on the line of the ball.
8. The head is well forward and down towards the pitch of the ball.

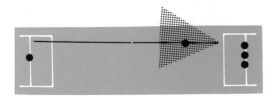

Fig 20   *Geoff Boycott, perhaps the greatest ever exponent of the forward defensive stroke, shows just how difficult it is to obtain his wicket.*

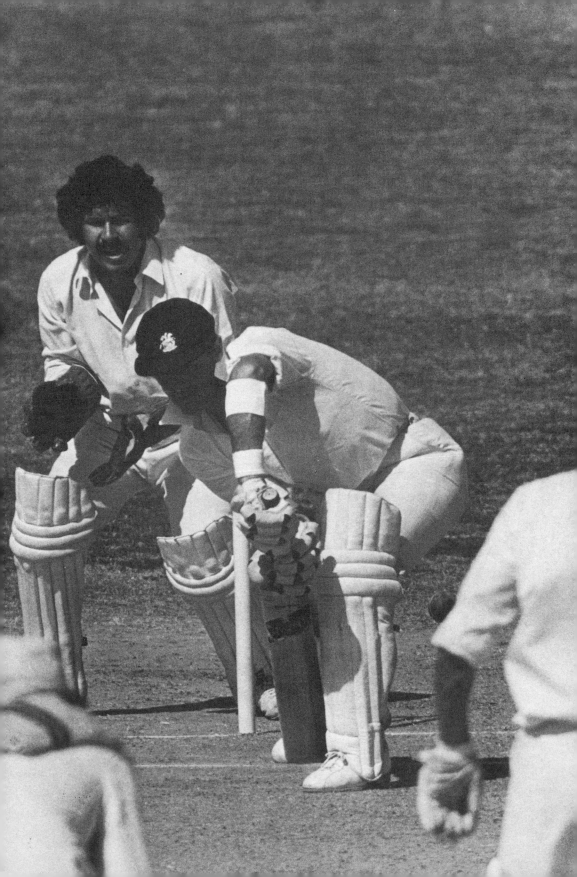

ATTACKING FORWARD STROKES

The Drives (Fig 21)

Whilst I am an advocate of equalising attitudes to back and forward play, I think it is fair to say that if you cannot play at least one type of drive reasonably well, then you cannot call yourself a batsman.

The Check Drive (Fig 22)

The name "check drive" has only recently been coined, although the stroke itself has been played, albeit sparingly, since cricket was first played. Almost certainly it was first played accidentally through batsmen using too heavy a bat. Bearing in mind that many young batsmen still use too heavy a bat, it is not illogical for us to analyse the stroke. In fact, experiment has shown that many batsmen find the check drive much easier to play than the full follow-through drive. It introduces a greater element of control, if not of satisfaction. It is, in fact, not very different in execution to the normal full follow-through drive, except in its finish. This is limited through a locked or checked wrist and a very high right-angled elbow joint, just as described for the check finish of the forcing back stroke. You should have the feeling that the power is going into the stroke through the back of the elbow. If you can play the drive with a full follow-through, do so — you will find it much more exciting. At the same time, learning the check drive will give you the advantage of a "second string".

Fig 21   Viv Richards leads with the front shoulder and head, the hallmark of the finest batsmen.

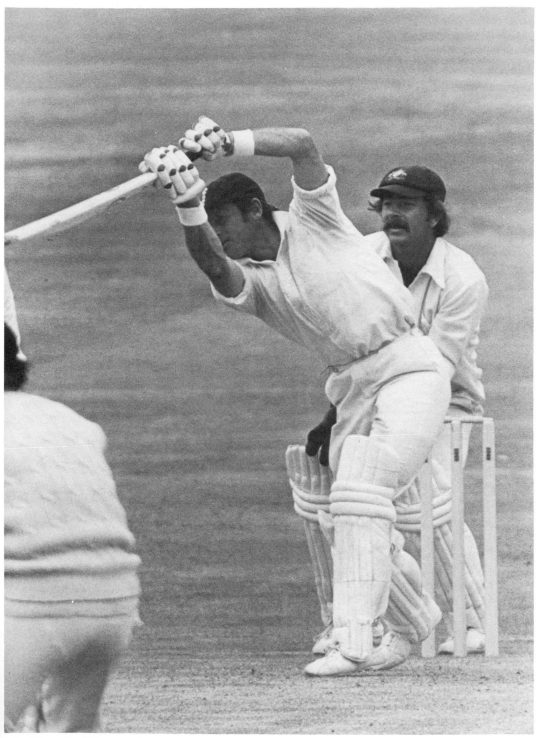

Fig 22   Geoff Boycott plays the check drive with
safety and the certainty of long experience.

Fig 23   *Sir Garfield Sobers – a tigerish off-drive,*
classical in every respect.

The Off-drive *(Fig 23)*

Played to:

A half volley pitched on or just outside the off-stump.

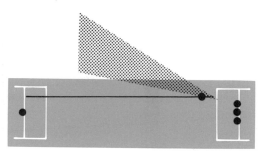

COMMENT

Technically, the off-drive follows all the initial movements of the forward defensive stroke, but with a very different intention in the final execution of the stroke. Recognising the opportunity of making contact with the ball on the half volley, the batsman is looking to accelerate the bat through the ball along the line of the intended stroke.

CHECKPOINTS

1. The front shoulder leads the front foot just inside the line of the ball.
2. The full face of the bat comes down the line of the stroke.
3. The eyes watch the bat hit the ball on the half volley.
4. The rear shoulder drives under the chin, giving a full extension of the bottom arm through the line of the stroke.
5. Wrists will lock for the check drive and break for the full follow-through, the hands finishing high.

Fig 24   Peter Willey cover drives with power and composure.

The Cover Drive *(Fig 24)*

Played as for the off-drive with a more pronounced shoulder turn into the line of the wider ball, which should be what you will recognise as a wide half volley. Avoid playing the cover drive early in your innings to the swinging or turning ball, especially on a doubtful pitch.

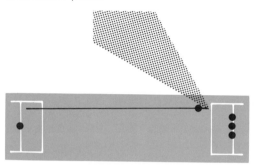

The On-drive *(Fig 25)*

Played to:

A half volley pitched on or just outside the leg-stump.

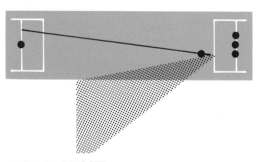

COMMENT

I have already spoken of the difficulty in playing this stroke. As in all driving, the shoulder and head should lead the stroke, but it is in the on-drive that the head seems to so easily fall over towards the off-side, causing the body to overbalance and throw the bat off the line of the stroke. A good tip is to drop the front shoulder slightly leading into the stroke.

CHECKPOINTS

1. As in all strokes, but particularly this one, stand tall, keeping your head well over your base.
2. Avoid hitting too hard.
3. Make sure you are well over the ball.
4. Along with the cover drive, do not try to drive the ball too square.

The Lofted Drive *(Fig 26)*

Played to:

A full length delivery pitching on or just outside the stumps.

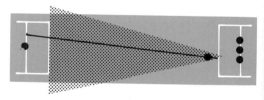

COMMENT

Lofted drives, whether they are off, on, or straight, should only be intended to be hit over the in-fielders into the open spaces of the field or even for six. Most batsmen would be virtually giving their wickets away trying to hit the ball over the boundary fielder.

CHECKPOINTS

1. Follow all the points for the full drives, finishing with hands high. No half measures!
2. Avoid leaning back. Hit the ball just short of the half volley.

Fig 25   Sunil Gavaskar, India's record-breaking
batsman, plays the on-drive with the
technique of the master batsman. Only the
very best players can play this stroke
properly.

Fig 26   Graham Gooch remains perfectly balanced
whilst hitting a magnificent straight six.

Moving out to Drive
(Fig 27)

There is one common factor that shows itself clearly in all good batsmen – correct and quick footwork. Being in the right position to execute a stroke is an essential part of batsmanship. If you are not in the right position, you cannot play the stroke; it is as simple as that. Once a bowler knows that he is bowling to a batsman who can use his feet, his tactics are limited and the batsman can more easily dominate. Moving down the pitch is a ploy that only needs to be used when the bowler has the initiative. The secret is in keeping a good balance and retaining the poise that is given by leading with the shoulder and head from a good stance.

CHECKPOINTS

1. Following the first stride of the front foot, the back foot moves just behind it, staying parallel to the crease to maintain the original sideways position.
2. The front foot is again lead by the front shoulder, as in the normal drive.

As an example; through the early sighting of a flighted ball, a good length can be turned into a half volley and consequently punished. If you do use this tactic of moving down the pitch, be realistic. If you have misjudged the length and there is the chance of you being left "high and dry", play defensively – do not go through with the stroke. Be sure to keep "in front" of the ball and do not throw your innings away, giving the wicket-keeper an easy stumping.

Fig 27   David Lloyd shows why some batsmen can play spin bowling better than others. See how he retains the correct sideways position even though well down the wicket. The wicket-keeper stays down well.

Fig 28   Zaheer Abbas, one of Pakistan's great
batsmen, plays a leg glance off the front
foot just behind square leg.

Leg-glance (Front Foot) *(Fig 28)*

Played to:

A good length ball (slightly over-pitched) pitching on or just outside the leg-stump, but going down the leg-side.

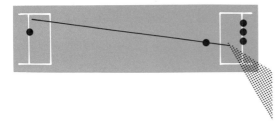

COMMENT

Take care not to play this stroke outside the body – it may result in a catch to the wicket-keeper. Neither should the stroke be played to a ball that would hit the wicket.

CHECKPOINTS

Commence the stroke as if you were playing a forward defensive stroke, but position your front pad to meet the ball if it is missed by the bat. Keeping the bat vertical, turn the wrists just before contact, keep the handle forward and aiming square on the leg-side rather than fine. The hands "flick" through a well-controlled stroke.

Fig 29   Mike Gatting includes the sweep shot in his
very full repertoire, which on this occasion
gives him a double century.

The Sweep *(Fig 29)*

Played to:

A good length ball pitched outside the leg-stump and turning in towards the wicket. The stroke can also be played as an alternative to the front foot leg-glance, i.e. to a ball pitching on or outside the leg-stump and going down the leg-side.

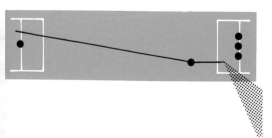

COMMENT

A modern stroke developed to combat the good length ball on slow turning pitches. Also it can be an alternative to moving down the pitch to drive, even on good pitches, when the occasion demands.

CHECKPOINTS

1. Commence the stroke as though playing the forward defensive.
2. From a high backlift, make contact with the ball just after it pitches, i.e. on the half volley.
3. Hit the ball down and direct it behind square-leg or finer if necessary.
4. Let the front leg bend fully, allowing the back leg to trail.
5. The ball should hit the front pad if the bat fails to make contact.

The Skills of Cricket

Running Between Wickets

Of all the methods of dismissal, none is more galling to a batsman (and his team) than to be "run out". More often than not, due to lack of experience, the younger the team, the worse the running between wickets. Matches can be won simply by good running between wickets, and this particularly applies in matches of limited overs.

THE STRIKER

Providing the striker has a good view of the direction and an appreciation of the speed of the ball as he plays it, he should make an early and clear indication of his intention by calling:

"Yes" for a run,

"No" if not running.

He should call "Wait" if he is not sure *closely* followed by "Yes" or "No".

THE NON-STRIKER

1. If the ball goes behind the wicket into an area where it is difficult for the striker to judge a run, the non-striker should then make an early call. This area is usually behind the wicket on the leg-side or when the ball is edged on the off-side towards the third-man boundary.

2. The non-striker should always "back up". That is, commence walking down the pitch ready to run, taking care not to leave his crease until the ball has been delivered, otherwise the bowler may run him out.

If either batsman disagrees with the call given by his partner, he should quickly call "Wait" or "No".

Both batsmen should run and turn as quickly as possible; the batsman with the best view of the ball as he turns should call for the next run.

Always slide the bat in at arm's length when completing a run. Unless the bat or some part of the batsman's person is grounded behind the crease, he can be given "run out".

To obtain a better view of the ball when looking for a second or third run, it can be an advantage to change hands with the bat. Always run quickly. This can cause misfields, tires bowlers, and generally puts pressure on the fielding team.

NOTE

Take extra care when running for a misfield. Do not take risks unnecessarily. Call loudly rather than not be heard. A batsman can be run out off a "No Ball" or a "Wide".

BATTING
Questions & Answers

Question In order of importance, what are the ten main batting faults to guard against?

Answer You cannot really consider faults in any order; some are more easily corrected than others and some faults are not so disastrous as others. However, the following are the most common amongst young cricketers in my experience:

(a) A bad grip and in particular, a weak top hand grip.

(b) A backlift that will never enable the ball to be hit hard.

(c) A poor head position when driving, i.e. letting the head fall over towards the off-side.

(d) Moving too early, before the line of the ball has been sighted.

(e) Trying to play the on-drive without having acquired the technique in practice.

(f) No sense of urgency.

(g) Not realising the importance of a high front elbow for vertical bat strokes, both off the back and front foot.

(h) Lazy footwork.

(i) When playing defensively, pushing the bat face too far forward past the perpendicular.

(j) Not leading into the stroke with the front shoulder and head.

Question What eight tips might be recalled by an opening batsman, just prior to the match?

Answer (a) Leave the wider good length balls that you do not need to play at alone for an over or two, until you have assessed the pitch and the bowlers.

(b) Look for singles; this can cause bowlers to lose concentration.

(c) When playing against fast bowling "think back". You can always come forward after an initial back foot movement. In fact, a lot of

very good batsmen move into a forward drive having first moved back. The reverse is very difficult. I do not recommend "thinking forward" when playing against fast bowling.

(d) Be certain that all your equipment is in good condition. Nothing is guaranteed to upset concentration more than being conscious of some loose strap or tight shirt sleeve, or uncomfortable footwear.

(e) Acquire as much information as you can about the opposition bowlers, so at least you will have some idea of what to expect.

(f) If your partner and yourself have made a good start, be prepared to accelerate your scoring rate as required by the captain.

(g) Do not play away from your body; make the bowler bowl to you.

(h) Give yourself targets in terms of scoring and rate of scoring, but always have in mind that it is your job to get the team off to a good start.

Question How do I play against a spin bowler on a turning pitch?

Answer (a) Take care only to drive when the ball is pitched well up. That is, what may be called a full half volley. Even then, be sure to drive with the spin and not against it.

(b) On a slow turning pitch with low bounce, look to play well forward when you can. On a fast turning pitch with high bounce look to play well back.

(c) On the "sticky" wicket when the ball is turning and lifting, the bowler will be trying to bring you forward. Look to score by getting on the back foot if you can, and if the ball is pitched short and off line on the leg-side, look to be pulling the ball for four. Conversely, providing it is not an off-spinner, square-cut the long hop pitched wide of the off-stump.

(d) Keep bat and pad close together when playing forward, allowing the ball to spin on to the bat face. Also allow the extended back leg to slide across the crease to cover all the

The Skills of Cricket

stumps and give a secondary line of defence.

(e) Really concentrate on punishing the loose ball, which invariably will be the short delivery.

Question How would you suggest a batsman might go about learning to hit the ball harder?

Answer It is all in the mind they say, and to some degree that is true. Firstly you really have to want to hit the ball; no last minute prodding. Secondly, take a leaf out of the golfer's book in looking for club-head, or in your case, bat speed. Simple mechanics will tell you that you need a wide arc, or if you like, a long and high backlift. In practice, picture your follow-through as you know it should be. Work on strengthening your hands and look to make a solid contact through the middle of the bat. Watch the ball very closely and do not rush the stroke. Take a few balls and "smash" them into the side of the net to get the feel of hitting the ball hard. Try to maintain a good position as you hit the ball, making full use of all your body. When playing horizontal bat strokes such as the square-cut and the pull, endeavour to hit the ball at full arm stretch. A full follow-through is essential if you expect to hit the ball really hard, no matter what the stroke.

Fig 30   Derek Randall shows that even the best batsmen sometimes have a "rush of blood" and hit across the line of the ball. Derek gets too many runs to do this very often.

3 Bowling

Attitudes

It has been said that the last bowler to be knighted was Sir Francis Drake! It is true that the bowler, no matter how successful he is, somehow does not quite excite the cricket loving public in the way that the great batsman does. Perhaps it is because the bowler, and in particular the fast bowler, takes on the role of villain, as, through his aggressive actions both physically and sometimes verbally, he intimidates both batsman and umpire. Perhaps it is the feeling of the batsman standing alone at the wicket, taking on all comers, that gives him the role of hero. Perhaps, and most likely, the artistry of the great batsman is more visible and consequently more easily appreciated than that of the bowler. Whichever, it is so, albeit through the wiles of the media, the image is changing to promote batsmen and fast bowlers equally as the heroes of cricket — and why not? There can be no doubt that recognition for a bowler is much harder to achieve physically, but in being so is more achievable, as effort replaces flair and becomes the catalyst which opens the door to any strong, determined and intelligent young player who has a yearning for the crowd's applause. Let no one think, however, that it is anything like so easy as a few words and dreams can make it sound. Bowling is a grind; long hours of net bowling, of physical training, of disappointments galore, when everything has been achieved but the catch that claims the wicket. Even then, some indefinable something has to be added to the effort; could it be subtlety?

One aspect of bowling that has recently taken a turn for the better is its coaching. At one time, all the coach required from a bowler was good length and line. Batting was the main interest. Not so today. The coaching of bowling has been recognised as a key to success and I recommend a bowler as much as a batsman to look for good coaching and advice. I am convinced that the time is close when success in bowling will again be measured in overs per wicket and not runs per over.

Years ago, I was very fortunate in spending some very happy times with a great man of cricket, Jack Mercer of Sussex, Glamorgan and Northamptonshire. Jack's career spans over sixty years as a player, coach, umpire, scorer, magician (member of the Magic Circle) and raconteur supreme. He played in the golden age, perhaps the only man alive today who did. His advice on bowling is worth recording: "Bowling is all about pitching the ball up to the bat, bringing the batsman forward". He also said to me: "When a bowler follows through looking over his bowling shoulder at the batsman, you can rely on him having bowled a good ball". Just two of a great cricketer's thoughts. I shall add one word — "planning". Plan your over, plan each ball, plan your net practice and if you are not approaching six foot tall and built like a tank, do not be disheartened. The best of bowling is for the spinner, the real artist, whose guile is essential to the future of the game.

| Fig 31 | The basic grip: batsman's view. | | Fig 32 | The basic grip: side view. |

The Basics of Bowling

In all instances, to simplify descriptions, it is assumed, unless otherwise stated, that a right-arm bowler is bowling over the wicket to a right-handed batsman.

Of all the skills in cricket, I personally envy the bowler's most. The bowler always, or nearly always, has another chance, whereas the batsman can usually only make one mistake. Another feature of bowling is that we nearly all can do it, or like to think we can. This is true, up to a point, in that bowling appears to be that much simpler than batting, although I do not suppose such a comment will gain much support from bowlers. To practise batting, a bowler (of sorts) is needed. To practise bowling, a batsman is not absolutely necessary. Bowling is more physical than batting and whilst that does not make it simpler, the basic requirements are perhaps more easily defined. There are, in fact, only four – the *grip* (of the ball), the *run-up*, the *delivery* and the *follow-through*. Of course, there are many variations on each of these basics to produce the different types of delivery, but these variations are refinements, not alterations, and take nothing away from the analysis of the basic structure of bowling that follows.

The Basic Grip
(Figs 31 and 32)

COMMENT

This is the grip from which variations can be made to give the type of delivery required. It is essentially a finger grip, rather than a palm grip.

CHECKPOINTS

1. The first two fingers lie alongside the seam, easily apart.
2. The inside of the thumb lies on the seam, directly beneath the first two fingers.
3. The third finger rests lightly against the ball, simply acting as a support.
4. There is a noticeable gap at the vee of thumb and first finger.

Run-Up *(Fig 33)*

Whether a slow bowler or a fast bowler, the same principles apply. The object of the run-up is to enable the bowler to move into the delivery stride with the balance and the momentum necessary to consistently deliver the ball with the maximum desired effect. I have found the run-up to be a sadly neglected part of bowling instruction, analysis and practice.

COMMENT

Rhythm is the key to a good run-up and this is what the bowler must constantly be trying to obtain. In practice, it is not uncommon for the coach to call out the timing. Check the length of your run-up and mark it clearly. Too short a run-up can be just as bad as too long a run-up. Time spent on establishing the right length of run-up to give you rhythm is time well spent.

CHECKPOINTS

1. Face the batsman; start slowly, gradually lengthening your stride and increasing your speed. Watch the batsman closely, progressively concentrating on the spot where you wish the ball to land.
2. Running at a very slight angle to the wicket may help you to "bound" into the delivery stride. That is, jump forward and high enough to enable you to turn fully sideways. Land with your right foot (for right-handed bowlers) parallel to the crease.

Fig 33 Michael Holding's long striding run-up is full of rhythm and balance.

47

Figs 34–39 Dennis Lillee – this unique sequence
shows all that is best in the great fast
bowler's action.

Delivery

(Fig 34) This is the heart of the bowling
action and is, without doubt, the major key
to success in bowling. Take particular note
of the "bound" which may be described as
the link between the run-up and the delivery.
As the run-up takes you into the bound and
hence the delivery stride, be conscious that
you are leaning back away from the
batsman. This position enables the fast
bowler to get maximum momentum
through the delivery stride. Remember that
up to twenty per cent of the speed of the ball
as it leaves the bowler's hand comes from
the speed of movement through the
delivery stride.

(Fig 35) As you land from the bound, you are about to go through what is called the "coil" position. At this position, the front foot is raised, the knees flexed, the front arm high, but not in such a position as to block the bowler's view. The eyes look over the front shoulder at the point where you wish to pitch the ball. Some experienced bowlers develop a personal point of aim to suit themselves. The bowling hand is held up to the chest, just below the chin. When viewed by the batsman, the back is slightly arched to achieve maximum height. When landing in the coil position, the lean away from the batsman is still very evident.

(Fig 36) Still in a good sideways position, the delivery stride (longer for the fast bowler; shorter for the slow bowler) is commenced. The length of the stride is important in that too short a stride will cause a lessening of the body action, while too long a stride can not only lose height in the delivery, but slow down the delivery stride itself. Note the open palm facing the batsman and the delayed action of the bowling hand.

(Fig 37) As the bowler comes through the delivery stride, the front shoulder guides the weight on to the left leg, flexed at the knee to take the impact created by the faster bowler, but braced following the shorter delivery stride of the slower bowler. When bowling fast, the wrist is cocked back to give maximum acceleration of the ball as it is released.

(Fig 38) The fast bowler's delivery stride is completed with the front foot landing virtually in line with the back foot when viewed by the batsman. For the slower bowler, with the shorter stride, the front foot lands slightly across the body. A high delivery position is basic, but it can be varied slightly, as required by the bowler's intention. The seam should be vertical at the point of release.

Follow-through

(Fig 39) A good follow-through is a must for all successful bowlers. The first follow-through stride is towards the batsman. The right knee leads the follow-through close past the left, without any splaying. The eyes are still looking down the pitch over the bowling shoulder. The bowling arm has cut closely past the left side and the left arm is taken vigorously through and well back, past the hip. Continue to decelerate naturally, still running as straight as possible down the pitch, bearing in mind that the bowler is not allowed to run on the pitch more than four feet past the bowling crease and one foot either side of the middle stump. Check this part of your follow-through in practice.

The Skills of Cricket

PACE BOWLING

Fast Bowling

The genuine fast bowler is a rarity indeed and to see the best in full cry is a special treat. Every young cricketer wants to be a fast bowler, but few have the physical gifts required. It is important to recognise the boy who can bowl fast for his age and, if possible, steer him carefully in those teenage years when so many are lost through lack of guidance.

The basics laid down in the previous pages cover nearly all the requirements of the fast bowler's action. Variations from pure speed such as swing and cut, can be added later, as can variation in pace and angle of attack. Proper fitness training, incorporating strength training routines, are a must for the keen young pace bowler. Good habits learned early will stand you in good stead later. For the young bowler who really has the potential to bowl fast, I should make that in itself the priority, rather than gear your action or thinking to swing or cut at too early a stage. Length and direction are important, of course, but again "think fast" first. Having said this, training should be tempered by good sense in taking care not to bowl for too long or trying to bowl too fast, especially when you are young and still growing.

Medium

Whilst the fast bowler is initially likely to concentrate on speed only, developing swing and other variations as a secondary consideration, the medium-paced bowler must concentrate on becoming an expert in one or more of the variations that should be a part of the medium-pacer's repertoire.

There are three main classifications of medium-pace which can be mixed, depending upon the bowler's ability. They are swing bowling (in and outswing), seam bowling, wherein the bowler relies on a very precise delivery of the ball to pitch on the vertical seam, and two types of cutter (off and leg), wherein the bowler drags his finger across the ball at delivery, imparting a degree of off or leg spin.

Swing Bowling (Fig 42)

Before looking at the action that produces swing or swerve in the air, it is important to realise why the cricket ball swings as compared to say the table tennis or golf ball. Since the seam was first introduced as a feature of the cricket ball there has been little variation in its construction. In fact, the seam is simply a result of sewing together the leather outer casing of the cricket ball. The stitches holding the outer casing together stand up from the general surface of the ball in such a way as to create a ridge around the circumference of the ball. By projecting the ball through the air in one way or another, the atmosphere, either dense or thin, exerts forces on the ridge, causing the ball to drift in one direction or another. Over the years bowlers have acquired the art of releasing the ball very accurately and presenting the ridge or seam (as we shall call it) to the prevailing conditions in such a way as to obtain maximum side forces. Consequently, the longer the ball is in the air, the more it will swing. This is not the advantage it may first appear as, more often than not, we look for subtle swing rather than a too obvious swing. Bowlers should experiment by varying the position of the seam slightly. Variations in conditions cause the ball to swing more or less. Variations in pace cause the ball to swing earlier or later in its flight. If

Fig 40   Michael Holding, one of the fastest bowlers
          ever, achieves the same magnificent
          position as Dennis Lillee (Fig 34) as he
          bounds into the delivery stride.

Fig 41   Bob Willis — not the classical action but Bob
knows what he is trying to (and does)
achieve in accuracy, pace, and bounce but
it is heart that breaks records!

at least one side of the ball is kept smooth or even shiny, the seam will have greater effect due to the difference in air pressure on the smooth side, as against the rough side of the ball.

The outswinger swings in the air towards the slips, when bowled to a right-handed batsman. The inswinger swings in the air from off to leg, when bowled to a right-handed batsman.

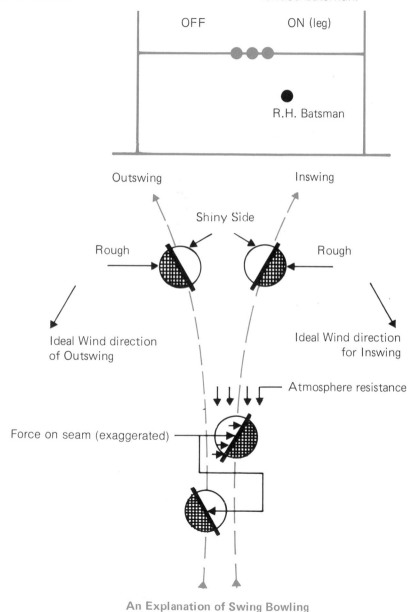

An Explanation of Swing Bowling

Fig. 42

Fig 43   Ian Botham – Ian's swing bowling secret is
that he retains this sideways position in his
action for as long as possible for both
outswing and inswing.

The Outswinger

THE GRIP AND ACTION (Fig 44)

The grip varies from the basic, in that whilst the seam is vertical on delivery, it is angled towards the slips (First or Second). The inside of the thumb lies against the edge of the seam. At the moment of release, the fingers should be behind the ball with the wrist firm. This action can cause a slow backward rotation of the ball that helps steady the seam for maximum swing towards the slips.

COMMENT

When bowling to a right-handed batsman, the outswing bowler should be pitching the ball on a full length in line with the off-stump or just outside, attempting to bring the batsman forward.

CHECKPOINTS

1. Delivering the ball from close to the wicket (i.e. bowling between wicket and wicket) increases the effect of the swing. If the ball is swinging a lot, the bowler can go wider on the crease to achieve the same result.

2. Angling the wrist rather than the arm towards the slips helps to conceal the action from the batsman, and in this way the arm can be kept higher.

3. Stay sideways as long as possible during delivery (*Fig 43*). Follow through vigorously, the bowling arm swinging across the body.

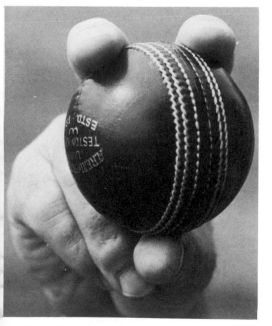

Fig 44   *Outswing: grip.*

Fig 45   *Inswing: grip.*

The Inswinger

THE GRIP AND ACTION
(Fig 45)

The grip varies from the basic in that whilst the seam is vertical, it is angled towards fine-leg. The ball of the thumb is placed flat against the middle of the seam. At the moment of release, again, the fingers should be behind the ball with the wrist firm.

COMMENT

The inswing bowler should be pitching the ball on a full length on the off-stump, bringing the batsman forward. If the ball is swinging a lot, it can be pitched up to a foot outside the off-stump, the bowler looking for the batsman's "gate".

CHECKPOINTS

1. In the delivery stride, the body opens much more for the inswinger, the back foot pointing more towards the batsman.
2. The arm should be high and the bowler should have the feeling of pushing the ball on its way.
3. The bowling arm follows through a little less vigorously than in the outswinger and may finish between right hip and wicket, rather than across the body.

Seam Bowling

For the seam bowler to be effective, the seam must project well clear of the surface of the ball. The skill of the seam bowler lies in the ability to constantly pitch the ball on the vertical seam, allowing the pitch, providing it is receptive, to deviate the ball in one direction or another.

The grip for seam bowling is exactly as described under the heading "The Basic Grip". The wrist position is very important at the point of release, as it may have to be inclined very slightly one way or another to obtain the desired seaming effect. Seam bowling is limited in application, as to be really effective, a "green" pitch is required. That is, a well grassed, slightly damp pitch, which acts as a resilient cushion to the seam. A good swing bowler can often use the seam very effectively. The natural finger action on the ball is a slight dragging back of the two top fingers at the instant of release. This has a stabilising effect on the ball. The good seam bowler relies heavily on variation in pace and extreme accuracy.

Cutters

The cutter is a useful variation for the swing bowler, although in the right conditions it can be the main striking force, rather than a variation. A soft drying pitch is the ideal surface with the dusty pitch of variable bounce coming a close second. The fingers cut or drag down the side of the ball, causing clockwise or anti-clockwise spin. Bowled at a faster pace than the spinner, the cutter's imparted spin has a lesser effect in terms of deviation. The following technical descriptions note the first or second finger using the seam as a wedge to cut the ball. Some bowlers bowl cutters with a normal spinner's grip, but in doing so, canno generate pace to the same degree.

The Off-cutter

GRIP *(Fig 46)*

Similar to the outswinger, but with the first finger wedged alongside the seam, which points in the same direction as the out-swinger.

COMMENT

The great advantage of the off-cutter as a foil to the outswinger is that once the batsman knows that you can bowl it, he is more likely to play at the slightly wider outswinger. When the ball is swinging, the good batsman can judge the swing so well that he can very often leave the good delivery alone, cutting out the risk of being caught in the slips or by the wicket-keeper. Knowing the well-pitched off-cutter may well cut back and hit the wickets, he tends to play at the ball rather than let it go, particularly as both types of delivery look very similar right up to the point of release.

CHECKPOINTS

As the ball is delivered, the first two fingers cut across the ball, the first finger pulling the seam down in a clockwise direction.

The Leg-cutter

GRIP *(Fig 47)*

Similar to the inswinger, but with the second

Fig 46   Off-cutter: grip.

Fig 47   Leg-cutter: grip.

finger wedged alongside the seam which points in the same direction as the inswinger.

COMMENT

A delivery made famous by two great English bowlers, Sydney Barnes and Alec Bedser. Being difficult to control, only the very best inswing bowlers can bowl the leg-cutter.

CHECKPOINTS

Everything must be just right at the instant of delivery, when the second finger pulls the seam down in an anti-clockwise direction.

The thumb helps by twisting the ball as it is released. Like the inswinger, the bowler has the feeling of pushing the ball down the leg-side. In fact, the bowler should look to pitch the leg-cutter on or just outside the off-stump.

SPIN BOWLING

If I had one wish in cricket, I am sure it would be for the compulsory selection of at least two spin bowlers in every team. This, providing that, having been selected, they would have to bowl at least half the overs that were bowled! What a game it would be; more overs, more runs, more big hitting, more sixes, more guile, more wickets,

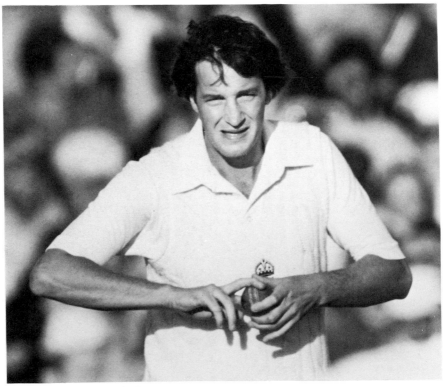

Fig 48   John Emburey is concentrating on more than his grip as he commences his run-up.

fewer maidens, more fun! In recreational cricket, of course, I think we do not do too badly for spinners, although one doesn't see the leg-spinner very often. I am sure it is all to do with the pitches we play on, but as these are unlikely to change much, perhaps legislation will come to the rescue. Nevertheless, I suspect that a lot of enthusiastic bowlers will continue to learn the art and get the supreme pleasure out of dismissing a batsman by guile and patience.

Off-spin

The delivery that pitches and turns from the off to the leg, when bowled to a right-handed batsman.

GRIP *(Fig 49)*

Fig 49 shows the orthodox off-spin grip. The first finger is the main spinning finger. The top joint of this finger crosses the seam. The second or middle finger takes up a similar position, the two fingers being spread as widely as is comfortably possible, to give the maximum spinning leverage. The third finger curls lightly along the seam, acting together with the base of the thumb simply as a support. The thumb takes no part in the spinning of the ball. Again, the ball must be held only in the fingers and away from the palm.

Fig 50 shows an alternative grip for the off-spinner, suitable for those with a small finger spread and young bowlers learning to bowl off-spinners. The first finger lies alongside the seam, using it as a wedge to exert the spin. Again, the third finger is spread, but will only be in a supportive role. The grip is orthodox in all other respects.

Fig 49   Off-spin: grip.

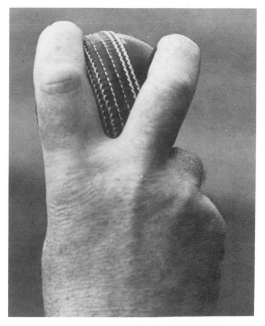

Fig 50   An alternative off-spin grip.

COMMENT

I firmly believe that to become a good spin bowler, you must have the ability to really spin the ball, even if you do not always use that ability. In fact, once a batsman knows you can spin the ball a lot, he will always have it in his mind and may subconsciously play for the spin whether it is there or not.

CHECKPOINTS

1. The action is basic in that it is classically sideways, with the bowling arm taking a full swing into a high delivery.
2. The ball is delivered against a braced left leg, the delivery stride being slightly across the crease and short enough for the bowler to "stand tall".
3. The spinning action is vigorous, simulating the right hand "opening of a door" and dragging the seam in a clockwise direction.
4. A full follow-through is as essential to the off-spin bowler as it is to the fast bowler, the right arm cutting across the body past the left hip.

The Floater

The joker in the off-spinner's pack is the floater. The best exponents of this delivery, in particular the legendary Jim Laker, have the ability to make it appear just like an off-spinner to the batsman. In fact, as the ball floats towards the slips, it can have the same effect as a googly by completely deceiving the batsman who can so easily play for the off-spin.

Fig 51   The floater: grip.

GRIP *(Fig 51)*

Very similar to the alternative off-spin grip but with the thumb located behind the ball on delivery.

COMMENT

This is an action that should be experimented with in an effort to deceive the batsman. Instead of the spinning finger dragging the seam in a clockwise direction, it pushes the ball towards the slips. A variation on the floater lets the first finger slide round and under the ball as it leaves the hand, making the delivery look even more like an off-spinner.

Fig 52   John Emburey's action accentuates the
importance of the braced left side in the
off-spinner's delivery position.

Fig 53   Abdul Qadir — almost alone as a world-class wrist spin bowler. Abdul clearly shows the importance of the strong wrist cock in this photograph. His open position suggests that he may be bowling a googly.

Fig 54   Leg-spin: grip.

Fig 55   Leg-spin: release as seen by batsman.

Leg-spin (Fig 53)

The leg-break is a delivery that turns from leg to off when bowled to a right-handed batsman by a right-handed bowler. Along with the very fast bowler, the leg-spin bowler is the most exciting bowler in cricket. Essentially an attacking bowler, on good wickets there can be no more effective bowler for breaking a stand or dismissing the top-class batsman when well set.

Unfortunately, it can be an expensive art to learn and very often precludes the talented young bowler from progressing as he should. Every captain must at some time have wished for a leg-spin bowler in the team when being held up by a tail-end batsman. There are a considerable number of variations on the standard leg-break and it is the ability to bowl these accurately that identifies the real match-winner.

GRIP (Fig 54)

The ball is gripped firmly and cradled in the first three fingers. The first two fingers are comfortably spaced apart, the top joints lying across the seam, similar in position to the off-spinner, but not so "spread". The third finger is bent towards the palm (at right angles to the first two fingers) and lies against and alongside the seam. This is the main spinning finger. The base of the thumb rests lightly on the ball as a support, taking little part in the spinning of the ball.

ACTION (Fig 55)

Prior to delivery, the wrist is bent inwards, enabling it to twist and flip towards the batsman as the third finger drags the seam in an anti-clockwise direction. As with the off-spinner, a good basic sideways position is established, giving a strong body action. The delivery stride tends to be longer than that of the off-spinner, but is still slightly across the crease rather than straight down the pitch. A high arm action gives bounce and accuracy, but greater flight and more spin can sometimes be obtained from a lower arm action. Once again, variation is a very important factor.

Fig 56   Googly: release as seen by batsman.

Fig 57   Top-spinner: release as seen by batsman.

The Googly

The leg-spinner's "secret weapon", the googly is an off-break bowled with a leg-break type action to a right-handed batsman. No single delivery can give more pleasure to a bowler than that which deceives the batsman into thinking it to be a leg-break when it is, in fact, a googly. The best googly bowlers practise long hours to develop an action that is as near that of a leg-break as possible when viewed from the batting crease.

GRIP

The orthodox grip is exactly as the leg-break (*Fig 54*). In an attempt to deceive the batsman however, leg-spin bowlers adopt two, or even three different actions for the googly, the idea being that the batsman may think the less obvious grip is a leg-break and play it accordingly. A simple action for accuracy is achieved by spreading the second and third fingers to grip the ball. The third finger is wedged alongside the seam, which it uses as a platform to create the clockwise spin.

ACTION *(Fig 56)*

There are two basic wrist actions for delivering the googly. Firstly, it must be realised that the ball must travel over the wrist as it is released either over the fingers and the back of the hand, or over the little finger side of the back of the hand. This is achieved by leading the delivery with the bent wrist, dropping it to allow the ball to flip over and impart off-spin with the third finger at the very last instant. To achieve maximum spin on the googly, the bowler tends to bowl from a more open (less sideways) position. This open position makes it easier to drop the wrist as the ball is delivered. However, the greater the change in action from that of the leg-break, the less likely it is to deceive the batsman.

The Top-spinner *(Fig 57)*

Another useful wrist-spin variation, in which significant forward spin is imparted to the ball, giving the impression that it gathers speed on pitching. One might say that there can be no such a delivery as a top-spinner, in that unless it is bowled with perfect forward spin only, there must always be some degree of leg or off-spin on the ball. I think, however, it is worth allowing the definition "top-spin", bearing in mind that the bowler should be looking for differences between the various wrist-spin deliveries. As in the googly, there are two types of top-spinner. In the high bowling action, the wrist bends and drops and the ball is slipped out of the back of the hand over extended fingers. It is almost a googly action, but the wrist has not turned so far. This may be called the googly top-spinner. The more effective top-spinner is bowled from a lower arm action in just the same way as a genuine leg-break. The difference is that the wrist is turned so that the seam points straight down the pitch and the third finger applies the strong over-spin.

Spin Variations

I first became interested in the possibilities of spinning the ball in different directions and with different actions when keeping wicket to the great Australian spin bowler George Tribe, and more recently after discussing the art with the well-known Australian coach, Peter Philpott, and today's leading practitioner, Abdul Qadir. Peter is probably the supreme authority on the subject as wrist-spin is a subject on which Australians specialise, although currently, it does not seem to be in favour with any country. Nevertheless, I am of the opinion that young cricketers in this country would benefit from developing an interest in this fascinating subject. Try using the grips that have already been described to simply toss the ball in the air. Try simple spin variations of your own and I am sure you will find the results worthwhile.

Another great Australian cricketer and broadcaster, Richie Benaud, dominated Australian spin bowling in the fifties and sixties using a wide range of wrist-spin tactics. I believe he had great success with a back-spin delivery that had the effect of keeping very low on pitching. Probably the most famous of the mystery deliveries was the flipper, which was perfected by three other Australian greats, Bruce Dooland, George Tribe and Cecil Pepper.

I make no apologies for dwelling on this subject, because if just one young cricketer learns to bowl the flipper with expertise, then the "sky is the limit". I understand from Abdul Qadir of Pakistan, that the ball is almost delivered as a normal leg-break, but at the point of delivery, the ball is released with a clockwise twist under rather than over the wrist with something like a snapping of the fingers, the second and third fingers virtually pushing the ball through with little spin. More experiment will be needed, but I may have kindled some interest for some young cricketer somewhere. At least, it may start some readers asking questions. Finally, for all potential spin bowlers, remember that spin without flight is like bread without butter or, depending upon where you come from, fish without chips!

The Skills of Cricket

TO RECAPITULATE

1. An off-spinner is a delivery bowled by a right-handed (finger-spin) bowler, that turns from the off to the leg-side when bowled to a right-handed batsman.

2. A leg-spinner is a delivery bowled by a right-handed (wrist-spin) bowler, that turns from the leg to the off-side when bowled to a right-handed batsman.

3. A googly is a delivery bowled by a right-handed (wrist-spin) bowler, that turns from the off to leg-side when bowled to a right-handed batsman. The difference from the off-spinner is that the ball is released with a wrist-spin, rather than a finger-spin, action. One might say that the googly is an off-break bowled with a leg-break action.

4. Off and leg-cutters are the same in principle as the off-spinner and leg-spinner described above.

5. An outswinger is a delivery that swings in the air from the leg to the off-side of the wicket.

6. An inswinger is a delivery that swings in the air from the off to the leg-side of the wicket.

SUMMARY

It will be appreciated from the above that it is the batsman that determines the description. That is, the off-side and leg-side are dependent upon whether the batsman is right or left-handed. Leg-side to a right-handed batsman is the off-side to a left-handed batsman.

Cricket is, indeed, a strange game, as we now have the situation that when a right-handed bowler bowls an off-spinner (off-breaks) to a left-handed batsman, whilst it is an off-spinner to all intents and purposes, it is, in fact, a leg-spinner to the left-handed batsman.

The Left-arm Bowler
(Fig 58)

Having looked briefly at the problems created by a left-handed batsman, the left-arm bowler, of necessity, must be clearly identified. The slow left-arm finger-spin bowler who delivers the ball with the same action as the right-handed off-spin bowler in fact bowls leg-breaks to a right-handed batsman (i.e. the ball spins in the opposite direction to the off-break). However, this type of bowler is not identified as a leg-break bowler. That title is reserved for the right-handed wrist-spinner. For purposes of identification, the slow left-arm finger-spin bowler is simply known as a slow left-arm bowler or a S.L.A. Generally, the slow left-arm bowler bowls round the wicket to the right-handed batsman, so that his natural spin forces the batsman to play at the ball.

We now consider the left-handed wrist-spin bowler. I am sure you will now appreciate that if this type of bowler delivers the ball with the same action as the right-handed wrist-spinner, the ball will spin in the opposite direction. That is, the leg-break will be an off-break to the right-handed batsman. The special name for this delivery is the "chinaman" and the reason for this, unfortunately, has got to be another story! A googly is a googly from whichever hand it is bowled. After these rather complex descriptions, we come to the medium and fast left-arm bowlers. In their case, I am glad to say that they are simply identified as medium or fast swing bowlers, depending upon which way they mainly swing the ball to the right-handed batsman. The left-handed pace bowler does, however, invariably bowl over the wicket to both right-handed and left-handed batsmen. The notes on direction in Chapter 1 will identify

Fig 58   *Derek Underwood – "Deadly" shows one reason why he is possibly the greatest ever slow left-arm bowler: a strong action, to go with his determination and supreme accuracy.*

The Skills of Cricket

the need for this.

In summarising this section of the book, I am reminded that no matter how simple we like to think this game of cricket, unquestionably it must be the most complex game there is. Maybe therein lies its fascination. I only hope the touring American with an interest in cricket does not pick up this book and read these pages first. Cricket in depth needs time to grow on everybody.

Bowling Tactics

FLIGHT *(Fig 59)*

Flight is another subject that is not to the foremost in general cricket discussion and yet it has a significant bearing on slow bowling. A flighted delivery is one in which the ball is projected upwards from the bowler's hand, rather than downwards at the instant of delivery. I am sure that it will

be appreciated that this presents another problem for a batsman in that he has to judge when the flighted delivery begins to descend. Only then can he begin to judge the length. Hence the expression sometimes heard on a radio or television commentary when a batsman is dismissed by a spin bowler, "he was beaten in the flight". A good spin bowler uses flight as a main weapon as he looks to produce the mishit drive from a batsman. A well flighted ball very often looks to the batsman as if it is going to carry further than it actually does, resulting in him trying to drive a good length delivery, thinking, initially, that he is hitting a half volley. The really high class slow bowler will even vary his flight by releasing the ball from different positions within the arc of his delivery. By letting the ball go early, rather than later, the ball will stay in the air longer, introducing yet another variation.

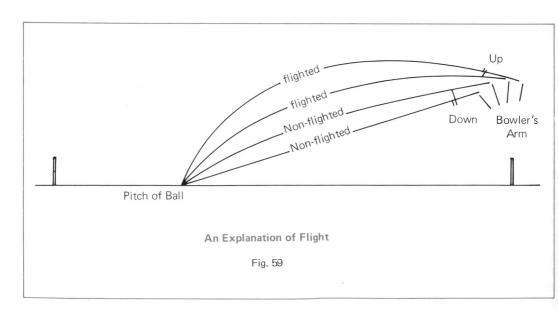

An Explanation of Flight

Fig. 59

VARIATION IN PACE

Whatever individual quality or skill a bowler may bring to his art, subtle variation of pace remains the key to consistently reaching the highest standards of performance. Whilst this is an obvious weapon for the slow bowler especially when related to flight, I am sure it could be used to greater effect by the fast bowler, providing that the variation is subtle. It has certainly been the success factor with the best fast bowlers in recent years.

ANGLE OF ATTACK

Angle of attack is relative to direction and is mentioned briefly under that heading, but it should be realised that the different angles can be produced in different planes. A slight lowering of the arm, for example, will produce a slightly different angle for the batsman to consider.

FIELD PLACING

Field placing for individual bowlers is one of the most important aspects of good bowling and good captaincy. It is underrated as a means of winning matches and receives nothing like the study it deserves from most cricketers. Over the years, standard field placings for different types of bowlers have been evolved and generally they work quite well in standard conditions against standard batsmen. The famous Australian scorer, Bill Ferguson, was responsible for compiling batting charts of the best players and I must say that I find it fascinating to study some of the great innings played by Sir Donald Bradman. In recent years, Bill Frindall, Test Match scorer and statistician supreme, has presented these aspects of cricket in a most interesting way. Cricketers should be aware that field placing in general is an untapped source of interest and information, and I hope they will be encouraged, as captains and bowlers, to experiment in improving their teams' results. A few pointers on field placing are included under the chapter on Captaincy. A general diagram, relating to the following specific diagrams, comes into the chapter on Fielding.

FIELD PLACINGS FOR DIFFERENT TYPES OF BOWLING

Fast/Medium Outswing (Fig 60)

The diagram shows a typical field placing for the commencement of an innings on a firm wicket with some bounce. If the opening bowler is very fast, adjustments can be made as follows:

Third-man (3) can move to third slip (A); mid-off (6) can move to fourth slip (B) or square gully (C). In this case, cover point (5) should move straighter to (D).

Only the very best of fast bowlers are advised to bowl to this attacking field. Generally, the original field placings shown in the diagram (1–10) are very suitable. As soon as the shine goes off the ball, if there is no movement in the air, short square-leg (8) may be moved to field at (E).

NOTE

The fast left-arm bowler bowling over the wicket and moving the ball away from the right-handed batsman, will set a similar field, except that all positions will be slightly squarer on the off-side.

The Skills of Cricket

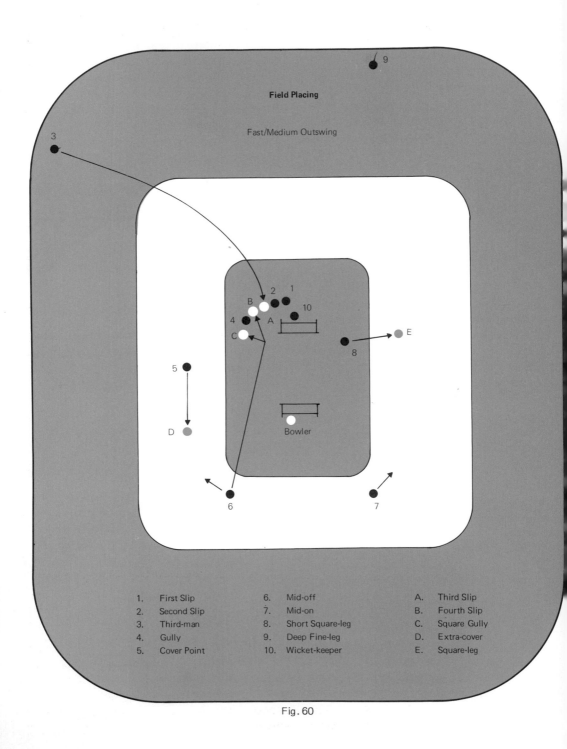

Field Placing

Fast/Medium Outswing

Bowler

Fig. 60

1.	First Slip	6.	Mid-off	A.	Third Slip
2.	Second Slip	7.	Mid-on	B.	Fourth Slip
3.	Third-man	8.	Short Square-leg	C.	Square Gully
4.	Gully	9.	Deep Fine-leg	D.	Extra-cover
5.	Cover Point	10.	Wicket-keeper	E.	Square-leg

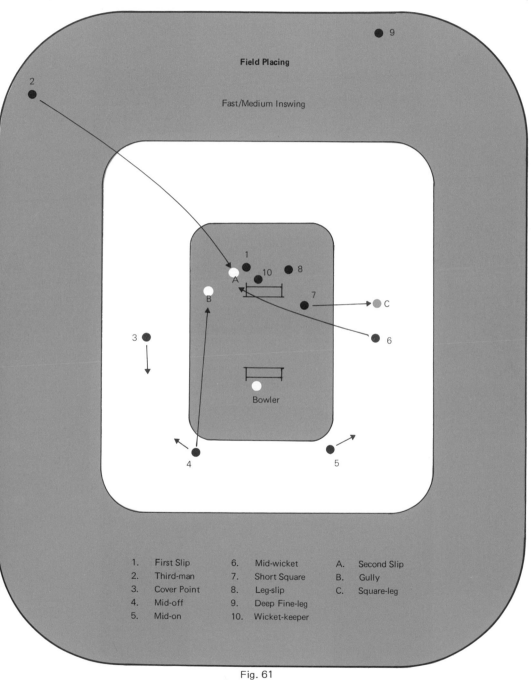

Field Placing

Fast/Medium Inswing

1. First Slip	6. Mid-wicket	A. Second Slip
2. Third-man	7. Short Square	B. Gully
3. Cover Point	8. Leg-slip	C. Square-leg
4. Mid-off	9. Deep Fine-leg	
5. Mid-on	10. Wicket-keeper	

Fig. 61

The Skills of Cricket

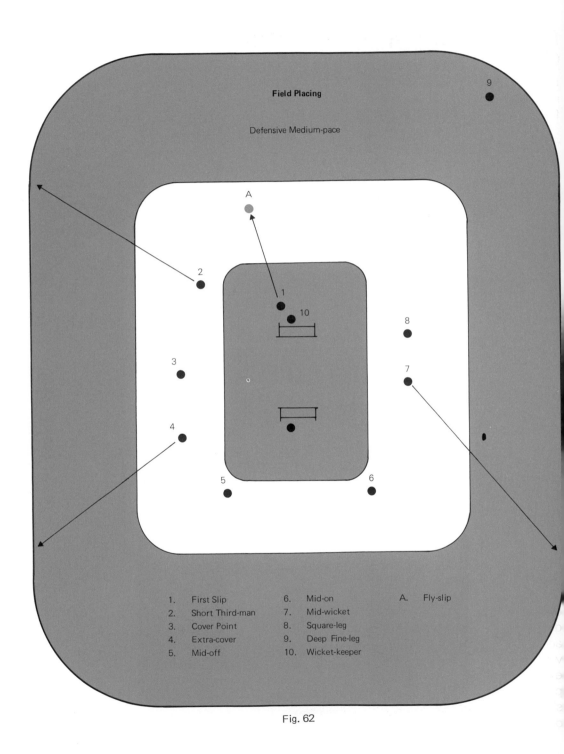

Field Placing

Defensive Medium-pace

1. First Slip	6. Mid-on	A. Fly-slip
2. Short Third-man	7. Mid-wicket	
3. Cover Point	8. Square-leg	
4. Extra-cover	9. Deep Fine-leg	
5. Mid-off	10. Wicket-keeper	

Fig. 62

Fast/Medium Inswing
(Fig 61)

If the opening bowler is very fast, adjustments can be made to the field as follows:

Third-man (2) may move to second slip (A) and mid-off (4) to gully (B). In this case, cover point (3) would move straighter. If, in the first few overs, a wicket had not fallen, second slip (A) would return to third-man (2). If the ball was only swinging a little, mid-wicket (6) could move to second slip (A), giving four on the leg-side, as against five. In this case, it may be good policy for short square-leg (7) to move out to square-leg (C).

NOTE

The fast left-arm bowler bowling over the wicket and moving the ball in to the right-handed batsman, will set a similar field, except that fielders on the leg-side will move finer behind the wicket and squarer in front of the wicket.

Defensive Medium-pace Bowling
(Fig 62)

In most types of cricket, it is sometimes necessary to bowl defensively, or change from attack to defence for different batsmen etc. The diagram shows a typically defensive split field that requires extreme accuracy for it to be really effective. In cases where defence has to be carried to the extreme, positions (2), (4) and (7) can be positioned on the boundary edge. Even first slip (1) can retreat half-way to the boundary, occupying the position of fly-slip (A).

Off-spin *(Fig 63)*

The diagram shows a typical field on a good wicket, when the off-spin bowler has just come on to bowl. If the off-spinner wishes to direct his attack more at the middle and leg-stumps, extra-cover (4) would need to move to deep mid-wicket (A), in which case, cover point (3) would move straighter.

When bowling on a turning pitch or attacking specifically, the following adjustments would need to be made to some degree:

Short fine-leg (9) would need to come in short, as would mid-wicket (7). Extra cover (4) would then need to be at deep mid-wicket (B) and point (2) would need to be at short mid-on (C). In some circumstances, it would be sound policy to move first slip (1) to the position of short third-man (D) allowing mid-off (5) to retreat to deep mid-off (E). In either case, cover point would move much straighter, almost level with the bowler's wicket.

Leg-spin/Googly *(Fig 64)*

The diagram shows a typical field for a good wicket. Extra-cover (4) may field on the boundary. If the ball begins to turn, short third-man (2) may be moved to gully (A) and extra-cover (4) to short extra (B). Mid-wicket (7) may be moved to forward short-leg (C). These moves would be made for a leg-spin bowler, only if he is extremely accurate, or if the batsman is defensive.

The Skills of Cricket

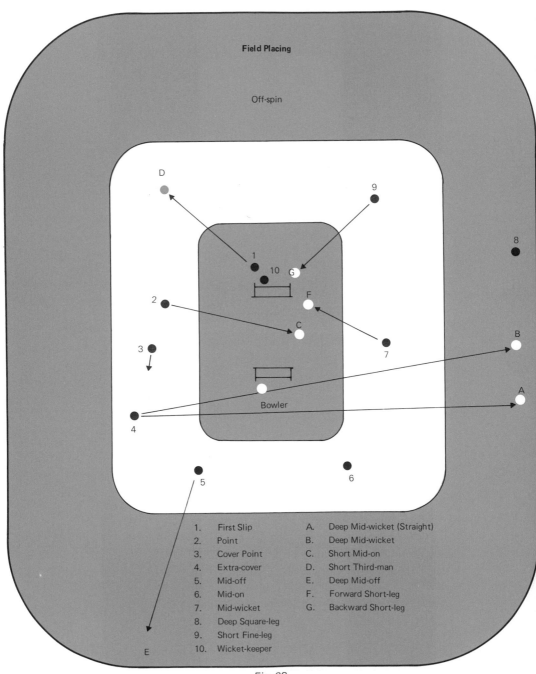

Field Placing

Off-spin

1.	First Slip	A.	Deep Mid-wicket (Straight)
2.	Point	B.	Deep Mid-wicket
3.	Cover Point	C.	Short Mid-on
4.	Extra-cover	D.	Short Third-man
5.	Mid-off	E.	Deep Mid-off
6.	Mid-on	F.	Forward Short-leg
7.	Mid-wicket	G.	Backward Short-leg
8.	Deep Square-leg		
9.	Short Fine-leg		
10.	Wicket-keeper		

Fig. 63

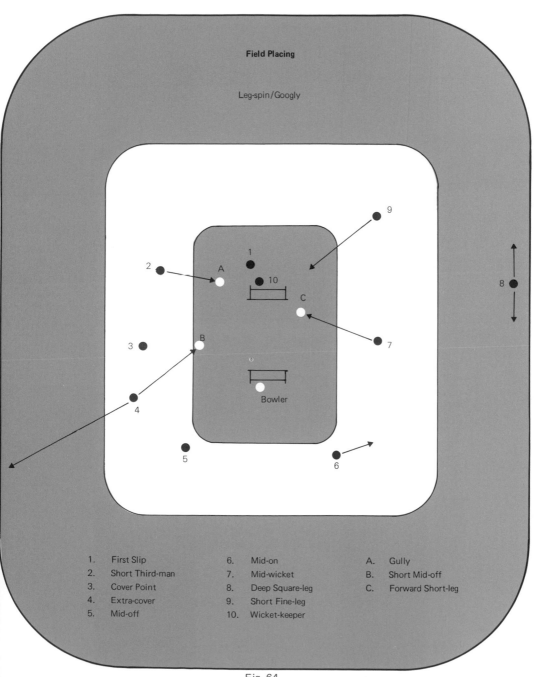

Field Placing

Leg-spin/Googly

Bowler

1.	First Slip	6.	Mid-on	A.	Gully
2.	Short Third-man	7.	Mid-wicket	B.	Short Mid-off
3.	Cover Point	8.	Deep Square-leg	C.	Forward Short-leg
4.	Extra-cover	9.	Short Fine-leg		
5.	Mid-off	10.	Wicket-keeper		

Fig. 64

The Skills of Cricket

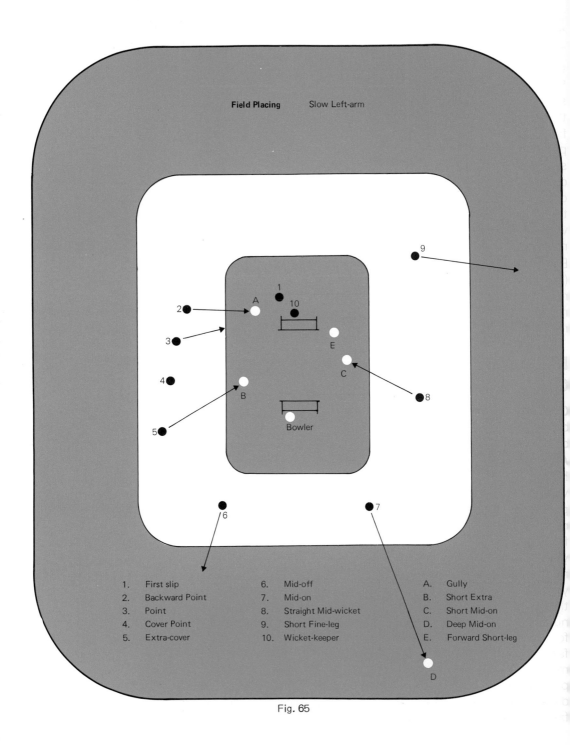

Field Placing   Slow Left-arm

1.	First slip	6.	Mid-off	A.	Gully
2.	Backward Point	7.	Mid-on	B.	Short Extra
3.	Point	8.	Straight Mid-wicket	C.	Short Mid-on
4.	Cover Point	9.	Short Fine-leg	D.	Deep Mid-on
5.	Extra-cover	10.	Wicket-keeper	E.	Forward Short-leg

Fig. 65

Slow Left-arm *(Fig 65)*

The diagram shows what may be termed the classical old-fashioned field for the S.L.A. on a good wicket. In recent years, slow left-arm bowlers have bowled more at the wickets and have invariably positioned a fielder at the forward short square-leg position for the bat and pad catch. This should only be a ploy for first-class and Test cricket, however, as I think this is a very dangerous position to occupy without protection of the head at least. On a turning wicket, the following changes may be made:

Backward point (2) moves to gully (A). Point (3) moves squarer and closer. Extra-cover (5) moves to short extra (b). Mid-wicket (8) moves to short mid-on (C). Mid-on (7) may move to deep mid-on.

BOWLING
Questions & Answers

Question What advice may be given to a bowler having consistent trouble with no balls?

Answer Almost certainly the bowler will have an inconsistent run-up, maybe with a variable stride pattern. A good tip, in practice, is to reverse the run-up. Commence from the batting crease and run away from the wicket. Try to gradually increase your running speed whilst maintaining rhythm. This means gradually lengthening your stride. Move into the bound and deliver the ball when you feel ready. Repeat this a number of times until you feel very comfortable with the run-up, neither running too fast or too slow. When finally satisfied, measure your new length of run, and practise in the nets varying your pace at different batsmen. Do not try to bowl too fast. Concentrate on accuracy.

Question A young bowler has lost his ability to swing the ball away from the right-handed batsman and is consistently pushing the ball down the leg-side. What may be wrong?

Answer There are a number of possibilities. Here are two:

(a) He is likely to be trying to bowl too fast. That is, running too quickly into the delivery stride and not giving himself time to establish a good sideways position at the wicket.

(b) Alternatively, he is letting the front shoulder and arm open too much, presenting his chest to the batsman. This often causes the ball to be pushed down the leg-side. He is simply not using the front arm enough as a guide to the bowling arm. The front arm should be reaching high and the bowler looking behind it over the front shoulder as he commences the delivery stride, and the front of the bowling wrist should face first slip on delivery.

Question Should a bowler sacrifice spin or speed in an effort to maintain line and length?

Answer Probably this is the most difficult question to answer in bowling. If done so exclusively, a bowler will never really learn to bowl fast or spin the ball enough. This is a fate that has befallen many good bowlers who have never reached their full potential.

Without reservation, I say that first and foremost a fast bowler must try to bowl fast within his physical limitations and through the shape of a good action. Experience and improvement in technique will allow him to gain better control.

The case of the spin bowler is different. It is only really necessary to spin the occasional delivery a lot. This heavy spin can be practised in the nets and in a match can be tried occasionally without disastrous results. Whilst length and line are important to every bowler, they are a lifeline to the spinner.

The Skills of Cricket

Question I am a medium-paced, swing and seam bowler and last season established a reputation in tying good batsmen down, but not taking many wickets. I feel that I should be taking more wickets, as I have a good pace and I am very accurate.

Answer Yours is not an uncommon question. Almost certainly, you are bowling between six inches and a foot too short on average. Next time you play in a match, concentrate on making the early batsmen play forward to every ball, even if you are driven for four occasionally. Once you can accept this, look for a more subtle variation in pace and angle of attack. I am sure you will achieve more success in the future in terms of wickets, if not in runs hit off you!

Question I am an outswing bowler almost exclusively. What other types of delivery would you suggest I learn?

Answer Every bowler should be able to bowl more than one type of delivery, if only for the fun it gives. More often than not, however, learning the second or third type of delivery properly also results in making a bowler much more effective. In your case, I should learn to bowl the off-cutter as a good foil to your outswing. Firstly, it can be more easily concealed as the grip on the ball and the delivery action will not be much different. Secondly, it will make your out-swinger more effective. That is, the batsman will not be able to leave your outswinger alone when pitched just outside the off-stump. There will always be the thought in his mind that it may be the off-cutter coming back into the wicket. On occasions he will undoubtedly play at the wide outswinger, as a result giving catches behind the wicket.

This principle can be extended to many types of bowlers. The inswing bowler should learn to bowl the leg-cutter. The off-spin bowler should learn to bowl the floater. The leg-break bowler must learn the googly and its variations.

Question What single tip can be given to a fast bowler?

Answer Vary your pace slightly in every over. Try to bowl a yorker with your extra-fast ball. It will give you and the team the greatest thrill when it shatters the stumps!

Question Which of the basics of bowling would you expect a young bowler to work on first for him to realise a rapid improvement in performance?

Answer The follow-through. A good follow-through can only stem from a vigorous action preceded by a rhythmic run-up. A bowler who is conscious of the need for a good follow-through will more naturally acquire the other basics.

4 Fielding

Attitudes

If there is one aspect of cricket that has changed in recent years, it is fielding. Now it is just as, if not more aggressive, than batting and bowling. Players are fitter than they have ever been; in fact, fielding at its best is now a spectator sport in itself. Players specialise in particular fielding positions, even differentiating between first and second slip, mid-wicket and mid-on. Without question, a successful team must be a good fielding side and practise together, as would a soccer or rugby team. A good fielding side somehow dominates the batsmen and makes ordinary bowling good and good bowling very good, as bowlers are encouraged, even "lifted", to give of their very best. Captains who study bowling tactics and field placing in depth are no longer in the minority and as a result, the tactical battle adds greatly to the interest in the game. "Catches win matches" is a saying that is proven time and again.

Fig. 66 shows general field placings. Specific field placings for different bowlers are shown under the chapter on Bowling. Points relating to field placing and captaincy are noted under the chapter on Captaincy.

Ground Fielding

Ground fielding may be logically divided into defensive fielding and attacking fielding,

which, in turn, may also be divided into either intercepting or retrieving. Timing and judgment are a fielder's natural assets when coupled with the physical prowess to run fast, and throw with strength and accuracy. When the instant opportunity for a run-out occurs, the ability to keep cool under the pressure is also an asset worth having, although this can apply in any part of the game. Some cricketers are born with the unique ability to pick up and throw the ball when off balance. Obviously gifts like this must be undisturbed and, in fact, cultivated. The best ground fielders only show themselves in their true colours when a run-out situation occurs.

Defensive Interception

This type of fielding can apply at any time, once it is absolutely certain that through its application a further run is not taken; neither is an opportunity of a run-out missed. There can only really be one defensive fielding technique and that is the Long Barrier *(Fig 67)*. This position is concerned with safely intercepting and stopping the ball as efficiently as possible and then moving just as efficiently into a sound throwing position. There is no reason why a run-out should not

Fielding Positions

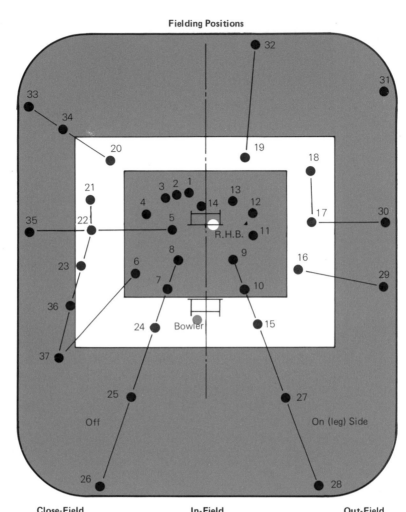

Fig. 66

Close-Field		In-Field		Out-Field	
1.	First Slip	15.	Mid-on	25.	Deep Mid-off
2.	Second Slip	16.	Mid-wicket	26.	Long-off
3.	Third Slip	17.	Square-leg	27.	Deep Mid-on
4.	Gully	18.	Backward Square-leg	28.	Long-on
5.	Silly Point	19.	Short Fine-leg	29.	Deep Mid-wicket
6.	Short Extra	20.	Short Third-man	30.	Deep Square-leg
7.	Short Mid-off	21.	Backward Point	31.	Long-leg
8.	Silly Mid-off	22.	Point	32.	Deep Fine-leg
9.	Silly Mid-on	23.	Cover Point	33.	Deep Third-man
10.	Short Mid-on	24.	Mid-off	34.	Third-man
11.	Forward Short-leg			35.	Deep Point
12.	Backward Short-leg			36.	Extra-cover
13.	Leg-slip			37.	Deep Extra
14.	Wicket-keeper				

Fielding

be achieved from this position with a good throw.

When possible, the fielder moves into the line of the ball moving right, if he is a right-handed thrower. The right foot is at right angles and behind the line of the ball, as the left knee bends fully to the ground just in front of the right heel. This presents a "long barrier" to the ball. The eyes watch the ball right into the hands, which are close together, fingers pointing down and just touching the ground. If the fielder has to move left and is a right-handed thrower, he still makes the barrier, only in this case dropping on to the right knee. From this position he takes one pace, pivoting on the right foot to achieve the throwing position.

Attacking Interception

The one-handed pick-up and throw from close in requires the fielder to move face-on to the line of the ball throughout the action. The throwing arm is drawn back only sufficiently to ensure the necessary speed of the ball through the air *(Fig 68)*.

From the longer distances, the thrower is looking for a two-handed pick-up, a good sideways position and a shoulder-level throw. Note the trailing foot *(Fig 69)* in the classic position for giving balance whilst picking up the ball. When speed is the main essential, and if the fielder has the ability, a one-handed natural pick-up and shoulder-level throw can be a winner.

Fig 67   The long barrier – David Gower.

Fig 68   One-handed interception – David Gower.

Fig 69   Two-handed interception – David Gower.

Fig 70   Retrieving: normal pick-up position – Bob Carter.

Fig 71   Retrieving: long throw pick-up position – David Gower

Retrieving

Retrieving will nearly always be carried out at top speed and consequently must come under the heading of attacking fielding. The pick-up and throw on the turn is ideal for the close catcher looking for a run-out from the in-field. For example, an edged ball, half-stopped by a slip fielder, can provide the ideal run-out from a fast pick-up and throw on the turn. The throw must be made as the fielder is turning and jumping.

The chase and retrieve from longer distances can be achieved by turning directly from the pick-up unless the ball is moving quickly. In this case the fielder's momentum normally takes his body a stride or two past the pick-up position and the turn and pivot are made as soon as a sideways position can be established. In retrieving generally, ensure that the ball is picked up immediately alongside the foot below the throwing hand (Fig 70). For the really long throw from a slowly moving ball in the out-field, a pick-up just inside and against the opposite foot from the throwing side is worth perfecting, i.e. left foot for right-handed throwers (Fig 71). When making the long throw using this technique, really push from the pick-up foot. This creates a momentum for the long accurate throw. I cannot over-emphasise the importance of practice and lots of it, if these techniques are to be mastered. The cricket games described in Chapter 7 will give you a lot of very enjoyable practice.

The Skills of Cricket

Throwing *(Fig 72)*

Of all the cricket skills, good throwing is the one most readily appreciated by spectators, whether it be from the out-field or the in-field. Probably the most exciting of all dismissals is a run-out achieved by inches after a great pick-up and throw. Accuracy, resulting from good technique, is all important and in many instances is the main factor in a run-out, although an early release of the ball is important in surprising the batsman. Also where run-outs are concerned it is important for the fielder nearest to the stumps to receive the throw in such a position that he can quickly remove the bails if necessary. All throws must be "backed-up" by the nearest available fielder to prevent overthrows at both the bowler's and the wicket-keeper's ends. Nothing is more depressing than a fielding side giving away overthrows from bad throwing and backing-up. Team practice can make this aspect of fielding worth watching.

There are three main throwing positions:

1. The long vertical overarm throw for distance and accuracy.
2. The shoulder-level throw from the in-field for speed.
3. When extreme speed of return is needed from the in-field, a one-handed pick-up is the most effective, followed by an underarm throw.

Fig 72   Derek Randall shows the value of the top-class attacking fielder. Speed to the ball and a quick, early release give him another match-winning victim.

Fig 73   Throwing position – David Gower.

CHECKPOINTS

1. Ensure that for both overarm and shoulder-level throws, the right foot (right-handed throwers) is at right angles to the line of throw.

2. The non-throwing front arm gives a direction to the throw, the eyes looking over the left shoulder at the target.

3. The throwing arm is taken fully back for the long throw, with the hand cocked, but for the quick early release throw, the arm is bent and the throwing hand not cocked quite so much. In some instances, for an early throw, all the movement is from the elbow with the body quite open.

4. Weight transfer from back to front leg is important to achieve throwing momentum.

The Skills of Cricket

Catching

Regardless of the position in which you are fielding, there are common essentials that mean success or failure in this most important part of the game. Just one good catch at a vital stage to dismiss a good batsman and the team can be inspired. One simple catch dropped can have the most depressing effect on a team. At the same time, everyone admires a trier and the fielder who makes a great effort to take a catch will always enjoy his cricket and give enjoyment to others.

The common essentials of good catching are:

1. Sustained concentration on every ball delivered.
2. Minimum movement of the head, at least until the ball is sighted.
3. Good balance.
4. Relaxed hands, slightly cupped with the palms facing the ball.
5. Only slightly flexed arms (almost straight) will enable the hands to adjust to the path of the ball more easily and allow the hands to give as the ball is caught. All these principles also apply to wicket-keeping.

The High Catch

Mainly falling to the out-fielder, taking the high catch presents a psychological problem, rather than any other. Sometimes the ball seems to be in the air for a long time. The secret is to consciously relax and do not move in any direction until you have sighted the ball. Once sighted, move into the line as quickly as possible. Establishing a good base is an important factor. Try to take the catch high, before the ball has passed the eyes. This allows the eyes to follow the ball into the hands and also allows the hands to "give" (Fig 74). Of course, this is an ideal example. If the ball is well wide of the fielder, it can be entirely effort and determination to get to the ball that counts and then, I am afraid, the ideal technique cannot necessarily be applied.

There is an increasing tendency, particularly amongst overseas players, to take the high catch in the same way as the baseball or skim catch. That is, with fingers pointing up, with palms facing the ball. I believe that this method is having a much higher success rate than the traditional high catching method. It is therefore important to acquire this technique (Fig 75).

Close Catching

It is in the close catching positions that matches really are won and lost. Together with the wicket-keeper, the close catchers have more opportunities of dismissing early batsmen than any of the other forms of dismissal put together. The close catching positions are those that really do allow for the brilliant and inspiring effort. In general players do not practise anything like enough to achieve the standards that are possible.

The three essentials of close catching are

1. Establish a crouching position, *equally balanced on the balls of the feet*. The distance between the feet is important - shoulder width is about right (Fig 76).
2. Concentration and the readiness to go for anything, preferably with two hands, but with one hand if necessary.
3. Close catchers should take care not to cover each other's territory. Staggered positions maximise the possibility of catches.

Fig 74   High catching: orthodox – David Gower.   Fig 75   High catching: baseball – David Gower.

Fig 76   Close catching – David Gower.

Fig 77   Skim catch – David Gower.

The Flat Trajectory or Skim Catch *(Fig 77)*

Fielders in the covers and mid-wicket, mid-off and mid-on, not to mention the close catchers, are likely to get a catch coming to them at an awkward chest or head height. These catches should be taken by simply inverting the hands, pointing the fingers upwards, but continuing to present the palms to the ball. This is sometimes known as the "baseball catch" and is a most effective method of catching a ball. In fact, it is the only way of catching a flat trajectory ball between chest and head height without jumping, which, more often than not, there isn't time for anyway.

Close Catching Positions

FIRST SLIP

A highly specialised position, usually occupied by the best catcher available, as apart from the wicket-keeper, most catches are likely to go to first slip. It is good practice in this position to concentrate on watching the ball all the time, from the bowler's hand to the point when the batsman has played the stroke. First slip must remain still until the stroke has been played. Do not anticipate.

SECOND AND THIRD SLIPS

These positions need all the qualities of the first slip. Most regulars in these positions watch the outside edge of the bat, rather than the ball, when awaiting the possibility of a catch. To avoid clashing when moving sideways for a catch, slip fielders should stagger their positions. Along with gully, second and third slips are probably the most difficult of the catching positions to occupy, as most catches come off a hard edge at high speed and very often the ball is spinning as a result of a mistimed attacking stroke.

GULLY

A brave position and one which can cause uncertainty as to where to stand. Gully must be in the normal position to take the hard edge and bat shoulder catch. If he catches a full-blooded slash, that must be a bonus. On occasions, and for certain batsmen, gully can drop back a yard or two, with the special intention of trying to catch the slash or slightly mishit square-cut or cover drive. On no account must gully anticipate a catch. Concentrate on watching the bat. Experienced gully fielders are also aware of a batsman's foot movements.

SILLY POINT, SILLY MID-OFF AND SILLY MID-ON

These positions are only utilised in exceptional circumstances. That is, for a new batsman, or when the fielding team have runs to spare and are trying to put pressure on a batsman. Silly positions are also utilised against defensive tail-end batsmen, or even to tempt a batsman into playing an unaccustomed stroke. Those occupying these positions should be ready to take evasive action at the slightest sign of danger. Keep your eye on the ball and do not turn your back on a stroke. Be aware that a ball hit against the spin will tend to go up. This is a fact not utilised to the degree that it might be.

Fig 78   Ian Botham uses both hands to make a difficult catch look easy.

LEG-SLIP

This position is very similar to first slip, only catches will generally come from the inside edge or even the face of the bat. Leg-slips are usually specialists in the leg-side close catching positions.

SHORT-LEGS – FORWARD AND BACKWARD

Again, these positions are for the fearless. Short-leg fielders need to be brave, but not reckless. At the slightest hint of danger, evasive action should be taken. Short-legs are positioned normally for bat and pad catches, not full-blooded hits. The best short-leg fielders are crouched and poised

on the balls of the feet, ready to move forward towards the bat. Hair trigger reflexes are needed in these positions.

SHORT MID-ON, SHORT MID-WICKET, SHORT MID-OFF AND SHORT EXTRA

These are not quite close catching positions, but neither do they come under the heading of the in-field. Positioned mainly for the mishit drive, with or against the spin, catches taken in these positions can leave the hands very warm. These positions are a great nuisance value and can also persuade a batsman to go for the really big hit, sometimes to his cost.

The In-field

Fielders in these positions need to be very quick off the mark, as it is their job to cut off the singles and fours, pressurising the batsman into making more vigorous and risky strokes. All in-fielders give themselves a few yards to walk in towards the batsman as the bowler commences his run-up. This puts them on their toes ready to move quickly in any direction. In-fielders, if they are to err in positioning themselves, should do so to benefit their "strong" side. A common fault with in-fielders is to move in too close towards the batsman. That is, being too intent on saving the single but in fact failing to save the four.

COVER POINT

This position is usually occupied by the best ground fielder in the team. On a good pitch it is the busiest position and a good cover point can save hundreds of runs in a season. Lots of practice is essential, moving both to left and right. Cover point, together with mid-wicket, probably run out more batsmen than all the other positions on the field together. It is essential, therefore, that the ball can be picked up equally well with either hand, whilst running at speed. The ability to release the ball early, sometimes when off balance, is a great asset. A fast and accurate throw, if necessary underarm, complete a picture that makes cover point a vital position in any team. Mishit drives very often result in cover point having to take the awkward head-high skim or flat trajectory catch. Be prepared for this type of catch swinging a little in the air as a result of the "sliced" stroke.

EXTRA-COVER

This position is well described in that more often than not it is a reinforcement or even a seal to the off-side field. All the qualities of a cover point are needed.

MID-OFF AND MID-ON

Over the years both these positions have been underrated in their usefulness. They have tended to be "rest" positions for bowlers, or the captain's position, from which communications with the bowler are more easily accomplished. It is true that they are ideal for a captain, but, in fact, both positions are just as important to the in-fielding role of cutting off the singles. Batsmen, early in their innings particularly, are looking to push a single wide of mid-on or mid-off and, of course, this is when they are at their most vulnerable. Both positions are likely to be the recipients of hard-hit drives and catches. It is perhaps worth mentioning that when a fast bowler is in operation, the wide mid-on, very often the only fielder in front of the wicket on the leg-side, is in a key position.

MID-WICKET

As with cover point on the off-side of the wicket, mid-wicket is, perhaps, the busiest position on the leg-side, needing all the qualities of a cover point with, perhaps, the extra resilience in the hands to catch a full-blooded pull stroke. Mid-wicket, together with cover point, may be allowed the luxury of anticipation occasionally, as they can very often see the batsman directing a stroke to steal a single.

The Skills of Cricket

SQUARE-LEG

Whilst this position should not be over-employed if the bowlers are doing their job, square-leg needs to have courage above all else. It is square-leg who has the task of not only cutting off the single, but stopping or catching the result of a long hop or leg-side full toss. It is very difficult to pick up the line and speed of the ball from a position square with the wicket at the best of times. When hit with full power, it can be impossible – nearly! Square-leg is also in the awkward position of being the person the bowler mostly likes to think has wandered out of position. This, of course, is to cover his own embarrassment when bowling badly. Captains should be sympathetic to square-legs!

SHORT THIRD-MAN

Another underrated position, from which a surprising number of run-outs are made. Fielders and captains need to carefully assess the conditions of the ground and the pitch before finally establishing the exact position that short third-man should field for any bowler. Short third needs special attention and experience counts for much. Invariably in dry conditions the ball will swerve at speed along the ground, particularly from the slightly mishit square-cut and as can be imagined, this can be most disconcerting when running quickly on to the ball. The swerve, fortunately, is always in the same direction, from square to fine, and therefore can be allowed for.

The Out-field

The out-fielder may be defined as the fielder who, because of his position in the field, must accept the single, but no other scoring figure. The out-fielder's main job is to dissuade the batsman from taking the extra run and if he does, give him a "run for his money". There can be no such thing as an easy catch in the out-field. Early positioning is essential, both in stopping the ball or making a catch. Out-fielders need to practise as much as anyone. Good throwing can give them their share of run-outs. Out-fielders must avoid the temptation to vary their position, particularly in walking in away from the boundary edge. It is much easier to make ground towards a catch, as against having to turn and attempt the catch coming over your shoulder. At the same time, the out-fielder may need to establish a position well in from the boundary edge, when that boundary is a particularly long one. Common sense will prevail, but it must be disheartening for an out-fielder to see a ball hit over his head and bounce inside the boundary. The out-fielder or boundary fielder, as the position was once described, should be a very fast runner. Unfortunately, too often the position becomes a home for the tired fast bowler, or should I say it did, as nowadays, with top-class fielding in all departments being an essential for good teams, fast bowlers are looking to become specialist close fielders for obvious reasons.

WICKET-KEEPING

There is a saying that wicket-keepers are born and not made. This may be true of the great wicket-keepers, but there is no doubt that the acquiring of sound techniques through hard practice can go a long way towards helping any enthusiastic young wicket-keeper to reach a very high standard of performance. There is no such thing as a bad wicket-keeper, at least not for very long, as he would be such a liability to the team as to make it an embarrassment for all and particularly the player concerned. This does not mean that a wicket-keeper cannot have a bad match occasionally. They all do, but somehow seem to bounce back and continue to enjoy their very full part in the game. A natural ability to catch the ball is a great asset to the aspiring wicket-keeper, as is the mobility achieved through a high level of physical fitness. A sense of humour is also of great benefit to the wicket-keeper in his position at the "centre of things". He can so often lift the team when the game is going against them and even afterwards in the dressing-room, he can play his part.

EQUIPMENT

Wicket-keeping equipment plays a much more important role in performance than is generally realised, particularly in so far as the gloves are concerned. Most of the wicket-keeper's equipment can be compared to that of the batsman's, with the exception of the wicket-keeping gloves and inners. It is for this reason that I am considering gloves and inner gloves in this section.

Gloves are probably the single item that can reduce a Test Match wicket-keeper to the lowest possible level, if they are not properly selected and cared for. I have often seen a young school wicket-keeper being given the job of catching the ball in a pair of something resembling boards rather than gloves. After a winter in cold storage, it is, of course, not surprising that they are not in the best condition, if they have not been prepared for the task ahead. It is important that the main gloves should be large enough to comfortably house inner gloved hands and still allow room to easily remove the glove from the throwing hand, if necessary. Both gloves, when new, should be lightly "hammered" in the palm with the bottom of a bat to develop the catching "cup". This should also be implemented by a lot of simple catching practice. The surface of the palm should be faced with soft pimpled rubber. Take care to replace this surface from time to time as it tends to become smooth and worn. Keep both gloves pliable, using leather dressing on the backs and cuffs. Too much packing in the palm of the gloves can result in a lack of "feel" when taking the ball. As in all equipment, lightness is vital for the speed of movement required by the hands. Inner gloves, preferably chamois, although cotton is as good, if not as durable, are an essential and sometimes an under-considered part of the wicket-keeper's gear. Many 'keepers bind the top finger joints with surgical tape over the inner gloves to create a finger stall that fits comfortably into the fingers of the main glove. If the inner gloves are not elasticated at the wrist, it is good practice to use a not too tight elastic band to give the compactness that will enable the main glove to be removed easily. Some wicket-keepers wet their chamois inners from habit – but the main reason for wetting the inners is to

Fig 79   The stance of one of England's many great
          wicket-keepers – Alan Knott.

remove stiffness from the material usually caused from perspiration in their last outing. Other special points relating to wicket-keeping equipment are:

1. Do not use too long a spike in your cricket boots. They do tend to stick in the turf when turning or pivoting and this can easily be the cause of knee and ankle injuries.
2. A cap can be a useful means of focusing the eyes on the bowler's hand. It can also be a focal point for out-fielders. The wicket-keeper can sometimes get "lost" amongst the close fielders when an out-fielder is throwing from the boundary.
3. Make sure that you have the lightest of pads, with the ends of the straps cut neatly after fastening.

STANCE

The normal position favoured by wicket-keepers is the squatting position, the weight equally on the balls of both feet, spaced comfortably apart. The seat is well down, the knees well bent and the hands are close together, resting between the legs with the tips of the fingers touching the ground and the palms open and facing the bowler. The chin is well up from the chest, with the eyes level in all planes *(Fig 79)*.

POSITION

Standing up to the wicket, it is important for the wicket-keeper to be comfortable and to be in such a position relative to the batsman that the delivery of the ball can be easily seen. The inside foot should be no more than half a pace from the stumps when in position. Generally, the position of the inside foot will be in line with the off-stump *(Refer back to Fig 7)*.

When standing back from the wicket to the faster bowlers, a minority of wicket-keepers adopt a crouching, rather than a squatting stance. This resembles a slip fielder's stance, with, perhaps, more bend in the knees and hips. This stance is possibly useful to the less mobile keeper, enabling him to cover a wider range of sideways movements. The position of the wicket-keeper is the same, whether in the squatting or crouching stance. Again, when standing back, the wicket-keeper should have a clear view of the delivery of the ball, taking care not to stand so wide of the off-stump that he cannot easily take the ball going just down the leg-side.

One of the most common mistakes made by a wicket-keeper is in standing too close to the stumps when standing back. Some-times called "standing in no man's land", this is a fault that occurs at the highest levels. Equally, the wicket-keeper should not stand too far back, thereby allowing the ball, and a possible catch, to bounce before reaching the hands. The ideal "take" for the normally paced delivery is between knee and waist height, letting the hands "ride" or "give" with the ball from a hands forward position, as the ball drops in its trajectory. Correctly setting this standing back position as early in the innings as possible, certainly within a few deliveries, is very important, as the close fielders (slips and short-legs) take their positions from the wicket-keeper.

TAKING THE BALL

Having established a good stance and position, the next consideration by the wicket-keeper must be an intended taking of the ball, regardless of whether the batsman makes contact or not.

Fig 80   Bob Taylor, like all wicket-keepers reaches
         a crouching position when standing back,
         before he actually takes the ball.

STANDING BACK *(Fig 80)*

1. Move into your stance position late, rather than early and avoid getting "set".

2. Do not move until the ball has been sighted leaving the bowler's hand. Only the very experienced wicket-keeper should anticipate any particular action, whether it be by batsman or bowler and even then, it is something to be guarded against.

3. Most catches come on the off-side of the wicket, therefore avoid getting wrong-footed by a ball pitched on the wickets. Think off-side, if anything. Through over-anxiety, I once was wrong-footed in a Test Match and missed the catch completely. The batsman had scored eleven at the time – he went on to score one hundred and eighty!

4. Discuss tactics with your captain and the close catchers alongside you. Decide whether or not you wish first slip or first leg-slip to stand wide, giving you the opportunity of going for every possible catch. Remember, two hands are better than one and that one hand is better than none *(Fig 81)*.

5. Look to getting behind the line of the ball, but be ready to sway off line if the ball comes to you at an awkward height.

6. After taking the ball, look to giving a quick easy catch to a nearby fielder, so that in turn, he can transfer it back to the bowler quickly.

Fig 81 *Rod Marsh, Australia's record-breaker, has changed direction to make this brilliant one-handed catch in the 1977 Centenary Test Match at Melbourne.*

Fig 82 Bob Taylor – normal off-side take. Bob still retains his position with his left foot and weight close to the stumps.

Fig 83 Bob Taylor – the wicket-keeper's classic accomplishment is the leg-side stumping position.

102

STANDING UP TO THE WICKET *(Refer back to Fig 7)*

1. As when standing back, move into your stance late, rather than early, to avoid getting "set".
2. Take extra care not to move too early. That is, be certain that you have picked up the trajectory and line of the ball before moving – and then move quickly!
3. Come up with the bounce of the ball, not before.
4. Try to ignore any movement of the batsman and consider every ball to be yours.
5. Get behind the line of the ball, particularly when it is over-pitched. Be ready to move off the line of the short-pitched or good length delivery. This will enable you to "ride" with the ball if it lifts off a length or bounces higher or lower than expected *(Fig 82)*.
6. Prepare to take the ball with the arms almost straight and relaxed. This allows the elbows to bend with the take. This is particularly so when taking the ball on the leg-side. Keep the elbows free from the body.
7. Avoid jumping or moving up and down as you move sideways, either to the off or leg. Try to keep the eyes moving in one plane.
8. Do not move the outside foot back, unless the ball lifts, otherwise you will be taken out of range of the stumps.
9. Look to keeping the weight on the foot nearest to the wicket as you take the ball. Keeping your "weight" towards the wicket as you take the ball greatly helps the speed at which you can break the wicket *(Fig 83)*.
10. When the batsman is playing back, try to take the ball as close to the bat as possible. This greatly enhances the chances of catching a thick edge.

GENERAL WICKET-KEEPING ADVICE

1. Concentration is everything. Even concentrate on concentration!
2. Catch the ball naturally in terms of bias towards the right or left hand. For example, if the right hand predominates in the normal catching of the ball, let it – do not try to change this consciously in a match.
3. The wicket-keeper can greatly help the captain. He is generally in the best position to notice any possible faults in a batsman's techniques. He is the first to know when a bowler has lost his "zip". Perhaps, more than anything, he should know just how the pitch is behaving, whether or not the ball is moving and so on. Of course, the wicket-keeper must have some experience and knowledge of what he may be commenting upon and even then, he should only really volunteer the information on request, or if generally agreed on policy with the captain.
4. Sometimes it pays to stand up on a bad wicket, restricting the batsman's movement considerably. Conversely, standing back on a good wicket can pay dividends. This is contrary to common practice, but I do feel it could be done more in the team's interest.
5. Do not use your pads to stop the ball. Always try to take the ball in your gloves, no matter how awkward the bounce.
6. Always stay within striking distance of the stumps when taking returns from the field, again, no matter how awkward the bounce. Remember that most run-outs are split-second affairs and speed in breaking the wicket is the main factor.
7. Keep a cheerful demeanour all the time, no matter what the state of the game. You are the leader of the orchestra and nothing is

worse for a team than to see their wicket-keeper "down in the dumps".

8. Keep yourself fit by regular training (see section on fitness). Squash is a marvellous game for wicket-keepers, as it encompasses nearly all the movements required when played hard.

9. Practice hard in taking the ball from the most awkward bounces.

Fig 84   Bob Taylor sways off line to take this high bouncing ball with horizontal gloves.

Fig 85   Bob Taylor – the cool concentration of the world record holder enables him to achieve this "impossible" take.

FIELDING AND WICKET-KEEPING
Questions & Answers

Question I am a keen wicket-keeper, but no matter how I try when standing up to the wicket, I seem to get worse rather than better in taking the ball on the leg-side. Is there an explanation?

Answer Taking the ball cleanly on the leg-side is a hallmark of the good wicket-keeper. If there is a secret, it is in not moving too early. In your case, as you try harder and harder, so you move earlier and give yourself little chance of picking up the line and trajectory of the ball before you move. Try to stay on the off-side of the wicket that split-second longer, so that you can pick up the line and trajectory of the ball. Practise the delayed movement in the nets. After a while, once you have become accustomed to the pace and bounce of the pitch, you can forecast the exact position your gloves will need to be in as the ball comes behind the batsman. There are no prizes for the slow movers, however, in this exercise.

Question Whilst I am considered to be a good fielder most of the time, I never seem to run anyone out, even though I field at cover point. Can you give me any tips that may improve my fielding?

Answer You may have all the fielding attributes with the exception of a good throw and, perhaps, confidence in your ability. Try making a big effort to release the ball earlier, especially when a run-out is possible. Take a chance in a tight situation and throw off balance if you have to. Take special note of how the run-out specialists perform in first-class cricket. Note that in certain situations you might deceive the batsman by making an extra special effort to get to a ball that has previously gone past you. Clive Lloyd, the great West Indian cricketer, tells me that this is a ploy he has often used with success.

Question I field in all the close catching positions and I am what may be termed a reliable catcher. That is, I catch most of what comes to me, but I never seem to make a good diving catch. Any reasons?

Answer There is a lot to be said for the fielder who is a reliable catcher, but I understand your desire to make a spectacular catch now and again. May I suggest that you could be taking up too static a position. In other words, you are setting yourself too rigidly, probably staying down too long. Possibly you are standing with your feet too far apart. It is very difficult to dive from such a position. It may be also that you are standing too close to the bat. Practise diving catches in either hand from a fairly upright position. Give yourself a soft landing ground to practise on, otherwise you will soon tire and as you land, turn the landing shoulder under to break your fall, and roll.

5   Captaincy

The captain of the cricket team is the person who more than any other can influence the enjoyment of the game for both player and spectator alike. More than that, the captain can be responsible for the atmosphere within the club as a whole. It is a position of importance and responsibility and whoever takes on the role must be aware of these things and not enter into the position lightly. Cricket is all to do with the enjoyment of a sporting environment which will set standards of behaviour both on and off the field and will encourage all those that play to improve their performance, not only to give pleasure to themselves, but more importantly, to others. With this in mind, the good captain will lead the team in a manner that will earn their respect, as this is the only way it can be attained. Winning must be the ultimate of any captain, but not winning at all costs. The game is worth more than this, and there is no disgrace in trying your utmost to avoid defeat once the chance of victory has gone.

If you can cultivate an optimistic, but realistic attitude, your job as captain will be that much easier. The majority of people thrive on encouragement and an optimistic word from the captain can work wonders. This applies equally to the experienced campaigner or the club's newest and youngest member.

Do not feel that you have necessarily got to lead from the front, by scoring all the runs, taking all the wickets and generally trying to be everything to everybody. Teams like to be proud of their captain and their pride must come from the manner in which you behave, whether it be in your unselfish manner or your impartiality, your good manners or in the way you pass on your wide knowledge of the game. The way that you perform is also important, not so much in number of runs or wickets, but more in your appreciation of the game as it stands. If there is an example for you to set, it must be by your effort in the field. Discipline is important in a team, particularly on tour. Anyone can play a bad shot or drop a catch and neither warrants a sour-tongued comment in public from the captain.

There can be no excuse for bad sportsmanship from a player and the captain should make everyone aware of this. Only take a player to task in front of the team if all else has failed and after repeated attempts in private. There will be times when you can do no wrong, and on those occasions you can easily feel indispensable for ever. Equally, your world can be very bleak when all your plans go wrong and winning a match or scoring a run is a distant memory. It is on these days that your mark is left, for, after all, you can only be the temporary representative of those who appoint you.

On Winning The Toss

Many are the captains that have been labelled "genius" or "hopeless" by the uninformed, simply on the strength of their luck with the toss. "Win the toss and win the match" the saying goes and in many instances this is true. How can the toss of a coin have such an influence on the game?

Many factors can influence a captain's decision to bat or field on winning the toss. In general, the shorter the time allocated to a match, the less the conditions of play (i.e. the playing surface and atmosphere) will change and the more the decision to bat or field will be psychological and dependent on the captain's knowledge of his team's strengths and weaknesses. Some teams perform better chasing a total; other teams prefer to have their runs on the board. Sometimes, in club and schools cricket, when only one new ball is used in a match, a captain with a strong pace attack may choose to field first on winning the toss, to give his opening bowlers the advantage of the new ball. If the "boot is on the other foot" and the opposition have a strong pace attack capable of using the new ball to advantage, the captain must again give serious consideration to fielding first.

As the time allocated to a match increases, so does the importance attached to winning the toss. A psychological factor that applies to all forms of cricket and tempts the captain to bat first is the theory that in a tense situation (usually the last innings) a bowler is less affected by pressure than a batsman. Fortunately for the game, this is only a theory and is certainly not always the case. However, it will be appreciated that a batsman, realising that he can normally only afford one mistake, will feel more pressure than a bowler who usually has the luxury of another chance, should he make a mistake.

Having commented on the psychological aspects of winning the toss and batting or fielding, it is fair to say that in matches of one day and more changing playing conditions, mainly caused by weather, have the greater influence on the result. For example, when the playing surface is dry at the commencement of the match, the team batting first can usually expect the best of the batting conditions. That is, the pitch can only get worse through the effect of wear or rain. More often than not, a cricket pitch will increasingly help the spin bowler the longer the match progresses. The amount of grass on a pitch can also influence its behaviour. Very often a well grassed pitch will suit the pace bowlers. In these circumstances a captain can be tempted to put the opposing team in to bat on winning the toss. This is an infrequent occurence, however, and is only usually done when in addition to the pitch being "grassy", it is also wet and drying quickly, either through wind or sun. Captains should be most careful in their assessment of a wet pitch, as only when it is drying quickly can the decision to bowl first be completely justified, regardless of whether the pitch is well grassed or not.

In discussing the playing surface so far, we have considered only the pitch or the wicket, whichever one prefers to call it. In fact, the conditions of the out-field should be noted by the captain, as this can be a significant factor in his decision on winning the toss. For example, if a team have to bat on a slow, wet out-field after having fielded on a fast, dry out-field, they will be at an obvious disadvantage – a fact that should not be underrated. Remember also that a wet ball severely hampers all types of bowler, as does a slippery, wet run-up.

When looking to the weather as a guide to how it may affect the playing surface, well before and at the commencement of a match, the captain should also be aware of how the weather may affect the atmosphere. A heavy overcast sky will assist the pace bowlers, as will a humid atmosphere, causing the ball to swing more than it would normally do. Whilst this may

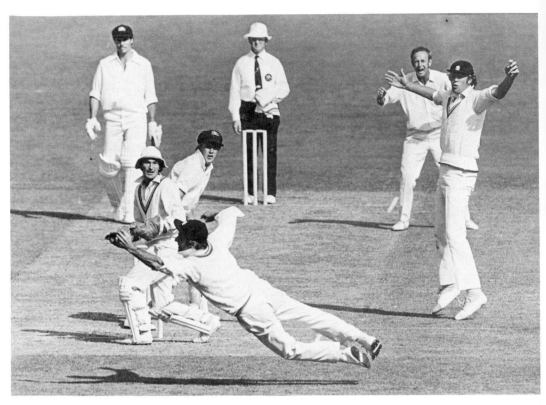

Fig 86   *Michael Brearley, an inspired captain, makes an inspired catch — which makes an inspired team.*

not be a strong reason for bowling first (the overcast sky may forecast rain), it is something to be taken into consideration when making the final decision. And so even with the knowledge and more, contained in the preceding notes, a famous Yorkshire and England captain once said: "If you win the toss and think about fielding first, think about it as much as you want, but make sure your team bat first". Whilst one need not be quite so dogmatic, reasonable advice to a captain would be — if in doubt, *bat!* Fortunately, cricket, being the game it is, confounds the best laid plans and both the best and worst captains have a happy knack of winning against the odds. "A good toss to lose" is a quote I have heard somewhere.

On Fielding

Up to actually tossing the coin with the opposing captain, there is generally little urgency as players change and sometimes practise, either on instructions or not. Once the toss has decided your fate, however, there is a definite change in the dressing-room atmosphere and tempo. When the team is in the field, there is a more collective urgency, even if the batsmen who had been mentally preparing to bat do tend to relax. This is the time when the captain has a very important part to play. In the time remaining before leading the team out into the field, you must wear a number of different caps. It may be necessary to give the team a "pep talk", maybe highlighting one or two outstanding tactical points. The team's different personalities will need to be treated quite differently, lifting some players and calming others. Some thought will have to be given to the prevailing conditions, both of the ground and the atmosphere. Which direction is the wind blowing? Is last night's rain going to affect the pitch? Is our star fast bowler really fit? A host of other thoughts will cross your mind before someone says "the umpires have gone skipper". Of all the experiences you may have in sport, I venture to say that there is nothing quite like leading your team into the field. Everything becomes worthwhile in the pride of that short walk.

The good captain will, of course, have done a considerable amount of pre-match planning. Everyone in the team will know exactly where he is fielding; both opening bowlers will have warmed up and be ready to bowl "flat out" from the start. The opposing batsmen will have been discussed and everyone will be aware of the plan of attack.

In the first over or two, adjustments may have to be made in the actual positions, as the pace of the wicket and the out-field determine the angles and speed of the ball leaving the bat. Throughout the innings, the captain will be checking the exact positions of all the fielders and they in turn should be watching the captain for instructions when the ball is dead. Constant contact, discussion, and encouragement for the bowlers will be a prime consideration. It will be particularly important for the captain to keep in touch with the bowlers who are not in action at the time. This will encourage them and make them feel a part of the game. The wicket-keeper can be a valuable ally in the field and a vital supporting influence to the captain. Everyone in the field should be in no doubt as to who is in charge and the captain will need to assert his authority on occasions, sometimes through controversial bowling or field placing changes. In fact, it is most important that a captain uses imagination and does not become predictable.

At the same time, common sense must prevail, particularly in the handling of bowlers. For example, the captain will, or should, know whether a wicket is taking spin or helping the pace bowler. Whichever, he should back his judgment at all times. If a spin bowler is in the team, he should bowl on a spinner's wicket, regardless of the fact that an outstanding fast bowler is in the team. Only in this way can bowlers develop their skills. Captains should take care not to over-bowl their main bowlers when conditions are in their favour. Many is the time I have seen a marvellous early performance on a "green wicket" by the main strike bowlers, only to see them "run out of steam" through being over-bowled in their first spell. It is a temptation that must be resisted and a strong reminder on the necessity of really knowing your bowlers' capabilities.

The hallmark of the really astute captain is in his assessment of the opposition and how any knowledge he has is used. The clever captain in the field will ensure that his bowlers' best efforts are concentrated on exerting pressure on the weaker of the two batsmen at the wicket. The whole team must be made aware of the importance of saving singles, especially when the stronger batsman is intent on retaining the strike. This is particularly important towards the end of an innings, when the difference in the abilities of the batsmen at the wicket is more obvious. Good captains are aware of the importance of not wasting time in the field. Different placings for different batsmen

The Skills of Cricket

should be established without exaggerated discussions.

Field Placing

Captains worthy of their name should make a study of field placing. It can be the most significant aspect in the success of their team. Here are a few pointers:

1. Study the style and temperament of each batsman who comes to the wicket. If possible, have previous knowledge of his style of play. Take immediate advantage of this knowledge and set your field accordingly.
2. Know as much as you can about the ground on which you are playing and how it tends to play in different weather conditions.
3. Know the opposing captain and his style of play.
4. Brief your team well as to the strengths and weaknesses of the opposition.
5. Recognise your own strengths. For example, do not set ultra attacking fields when you know your bowling will not stand it. Nothing gives the opposition greater heart than a really fast start to their innings.
6. The captain has the final authority on the placing of the field, but the best captains co-operate with their bowlers. In fact, the experienced bowler is usually given first option as to where exactly he wants his field.
7. Knowing all the circumstances, be exact in your field placings without wasting time. There is no need for it in a well-briefed team. If different field placings are required for different batsmen, the field should change quickly as the bowler moves back to his mark. Let your field ebb and flow with the state of the game. Never let it stagnate.
8. Remember, you cannot set a field for bad bowling.
9. If a fielder drops a catch or misfields a ball, a word of commiseration and encouragement will help him next time a chance comes his way. An angry word or gesture will do no good for anyone.

Field placing diagrams for different bowlers are included at the end of the chapter on Bowling and a general diagram, showing all the fielding positions, is included in the chapter on Fielding.

On Batting

There is an entirely different role for the captain to play when his team is batting, depending very much on whether it is the first innings or whether they are chasing a total set by the opposition. Invariably to begin with, he is looking for the early batsmen to set up a reasonable total as a platform from which to attack the bowling later. This will apply even when chasing a total against the clock. There is nothing like wickets in hand to give batsmen the incentive to play their strokes freely. The captain will, of course, have influenced team selection, from which he will have planned the normal batting order in advance. If possible, a left-handed batsman will be included in the first three or four. This causes the bowlers to constantly be changing their line of attack, having an unsettling effect on the inexperienced bowler. If one of the opening batsmen can be a stroke-maker of high quality, so much the better. If he is successful, the pressure is so much less on the later batsmen. The captain himself should be at least a capable batsman, enabling him to set a sound example and occasionally play an innings of note. Running between wickets is a very important part of the team batting effort and the captain should always be looking to set an example in this.

Occasionally, it may be necessary to change the batting order for tactical purposes. I do not feel this is done enough in all types of cricket. Neither is enough serious batting practice and coaching given to tail-end batsmen. This is hard to believe in hindsight and yet we still expect numbers ten and eleven to bat like masters in a crisis. It is very important that the whole team know exactly what is required of each of them whenever they go in to bat. The batsman who does not play to the captain's instructions in the interests of the team, should always be disciplined to the extent of omitting him from the next match or two if necessary. Everyone, including the captain, should be aware that cricketers everywhere will acknowledge that the game will always be greater than the player.

AFTER THE MATCH

This is the time when winning and losing is forgotten and both captains and teams get together, even if only briefly. The real cricketers will have been modest in victory and congratulatory in defeat. It is a time for captains to acknowledge the work put in by so many people behind the scenes; the groundsmen, the umpires, the ladies who so willingly make meals and so often play such an important part in the life of a club, the scorers, and many more without whom the game would not be the same. It certainly is not a time for recrimination, but for those who have not done so well in the game, a quiet word of encouragement for the future will make up for everything.

Later, when the players have departed, or as soon as possible in the days ahead, the captain should look back on the game objectively, thinking on what lessons he may have learned for the future and how he may improve his own performance next time. He must make a mental note of how he may help players in the practice sessions before the next match, and if the team have played away from home, it can be a nice idea to "drop a line" to those whose hospitality the team and himself have enjoyed.

CAPTAINCY
Questions & Answers

Question What are some of the symptoms of bad captaincy?
Answer (a) Poor dressing-room atmosphere.
(b) Lack of keenness in the field.
(c) Batsmen not knowing their positions in the batting order.
(d) Fielders not knowing their positions.
(e) Fielders badly positioned for every type of bowler.
(f) Team not informed on the game's tactical policy at all times.
(g) The captain not seen to be in charge, both on the field and in the dressing-room.
(h) Lack of knowledge of technique and sound tactics.
(i) Favouritism by captain.

Question What single word would you consider to be most important in defining the quality of a good captain?
Answer Motivator.

Question What other qualities might one be looking for in a good captain?
Answer (a) Flexibility.
(b) Imagination.
(c) Subtlety.
These qualities prevent field placing stagnation and keep the team on its toes.

Question What reason might one give when one of two equally matched teams seems to be the consistent loser?

The Skills of Cricket

Answer Four strong reasons could be:
(a) Incorrect use of bowlers, i.e. over-bowling key bowlers.
(b) Lack of appreciation of the way the pitch is playing.
(c) Poor field placing, i.e. no attention to detail.
(d) Variable and incorrect batting order, i.e. failing to make use of each batsman's potential.

Question Give an example of subtle field placing.
Answer Try to place the field to encourage the batsman to risk his wicket. A good example is to ensure fielders are straighter, rather than square, when the bowler is quite correctly pitching the ball up to the batsman. This leaves gaps square with the wicket and encourages the batsman to play across the ball. Also take care that the in-field is deep enough. Very often fours are scored through them being too close. A good fielder will make ground towards the ball very quickly to cut off singles.

Question Outside all the technical requirements of a good captain, what personal quality would you wish him to have?
Answer A sense of humour.

Question What might be the outstanding mistake that inexperienced captains can make in the field?
Answer Setting attacking field placings without regard to the position of the game and the quality of the bowling available.

Successful captaincy is very closely linked to attacking from strength. It is important for captains to assess the type of batsmen the team is up against, the runs he has got to play with and the state of the pitch.

6 Fitness

There is no doubt that the cricketer of today is much fitter than his counterpart of not many years ago. This is not to say that most cricketers of today are as fit as they might be. In fact physical fitness training for cricketers is a comparatively recent innovation. Together with practice, fitness training is an area that still has much to offer in improving a player's performance, although at the highest levels of cricket, I must say that fielding has become something of a spectator sport in itself. In general however, the lack of success from apparently talented players can very often be traced to a lack of physical fitness. Skills are at their best in their initial performance but can quickly break down under sustained physical pressure. Having said this, let me hasten to add that physical fitness can only play a limited role in the success of a cricketer. A knowledge of and an ability to perform the skills of the game will always lead the way and fitness as such will only ever be an assistance to maintaining the

Fig 87   Keeping fit — the England team warm up before a match.

quality and quantity of those skills. In fitness training, especially outside the cricket season, there is much enjoyment in players getting together as a group or team. Training sessions help players get to know each other and can only help to make the game in the summer so much better collectively as well as individually.

The importance of fitness can easily be recognised in any number of cricket situations. Just consider yourself, for example. Can you honestly say that, immediately after running the second or third consecutive three runs in an over, you are just as likely to score off or even survive the next ball with the certainty you did the first of the over? I doubt it and if the bowler knows his job I do not think he will be giving you much time to recover. What chance do you think a bowler has of bowling at his best if he cannot cope with a chase or two around the boundary edge between overs? How do you think the odds change on a wicket-keeper missing a catch in the first over through lack of concentration after he has batted for two or three hours just previously?

WARMING UP

When it is known that any exercise is to take place requiring maximum effort, whether it be in training or in a match, warming up exercises should be undertaken. This reduces the possibility of injury. The warm-up should produce a "slight sweating" condition through such physical activities as light jogging or easy general exercises. The light practice of fielding skills can provide a more interesting warm-up.

SPECIFIC TRAINING

Specific training like specific practice is the most desirable and effective training for a cricketer. Specific circuit training programmes can be designed by the coaches or the individual with a little experience and research. Specialists in physical education are always willing to help particular sports in this respect. This type of programme will bring a player up to a satisfactory standard of fitness without over-emphasis on fitness as against skill training.

CIRCUIT TRAINING (Fig 88)

Circuit training in cricket is a simple method of giving a player a variety of exercises that will improve the three main functions relating to his performance on the field. These are strength, endurance, and mobility. Circuit training suits the cricketer very well in that it is realistic and enables the player to keep within his physical capabilities.

PROCEDURE FOR ESTABLISHING A CIRCUIT

A programme is designed covering say eight exercises, each relating to cricket skills a player is likely to perform. Each exercise is practised until proficiency is achieved. The number of repetitions achieved on each exercise in say 60 seconds is recorded. This number is then halved and performed in two thirds of the time i.e. 40 seconds. The whole circuit may then be repeated a set number, say three times, trying to maintain the target time of 40 seconds per exercise. Players work at achieving this target time and in doing so build an increasingly better standard of fitness. When the target time is achieved the programme can be intensified by reducing the target time or by increasing the number of repetitions. Alternatively a new circuit can be designed.

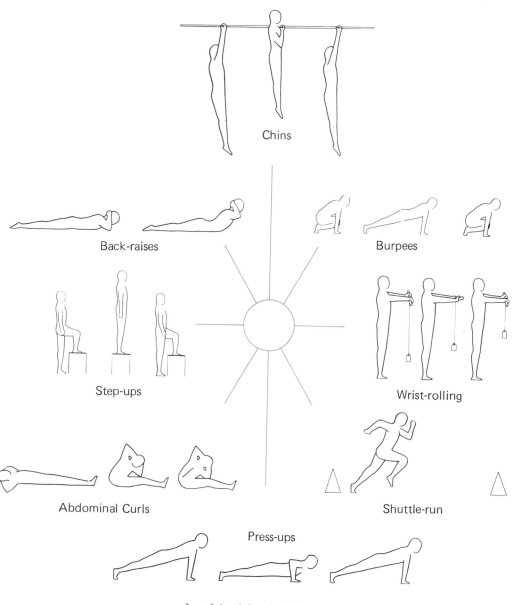

Chins

Back-raises

Burpees

Step-ups

Wrist-rolling

Abdominal Curls

Shuttle-run

Press-ups

A useful training circuit for cricketers
without the use of special equipment

Fig. 88

The Skills of Cricket

Important

If there is any reason to think that the exercises in a programme are too strenuous, qualified advice should be sought. In very fit young cricketers training can take place at up to 180 heart beats per minute. In general it is inadvisable to go beyond 150. Weight training should only be carried out under qualified instruction. Stretching exercises should be gentle and within the normal range of the joint. To improve the cardiac and respiratory systems the specific circuit training exercises can be combined with a variety of running activities, i.e. cross-country (2–5 miles), interval (short periods of rest), relay (in teams) and shuttle sprints (individual). In all training exercises involving rest periods, ensure that these rest periods do in fact allow recovery. Do not shorten the rest period unless they do.

Circuit for Cricket Skills

Depending upon the skills you wish to practise, select any combination of five from the following. Check your total repetitions on each skill and progressively try to increase the number in the same time over a period of weeks. Alternatively, keep the same number of repetitions and try to reduce the time in which they are performed. Complete at least three full circuits to establish a target.

1) Fielding – Close Catching
Make a chalk mark four paces from a firm wall surface and four feet (4') from floor level on the wall itself. From your marker throw a tennis ball against the wall as hard as possible beneath the 4' mark for one minute. Record the number of return catches you make.

2) Batting – Backlift
Set a string or rope horizontally at head height. Take your normal stance with your front shoulder pointing away from the string so that when completing a full backlift the bottom of your bat just touches the string. Record the number of correct backlifts you make from the correct stance in one minute.

3) Bowling Action
Set up two sets of wickets or larger targets 22 yds apart marking the creases at both ends with chalk. Take your normal run, select a ball from a container placed at the beginning of your run. Bowl normally, but after your follow-through run to the other end and repeat. Record the number of good deliveries (pitching on a marker) you make in one minute.

4) Running Between Wickets
Bat in hand run between markers set 20 yds apart touching down with the bat as you would in a match. Record the number of runs in one minute.

5) Fielding – Stop and Throw
Position a bucket of tennis balls a minimum of 30 paces from a firm, plain wall. Throw one ball at the wall over a height of 8' if possible, field the return in the long barrier position and throw again from the same distance. Record the number of correct throws made in one minute.

6) Fielding – Retrieving
Again mark at least 8' from the floor on a firm plain wall and make a large target above the line. Line up a number of tennis balls next to each other on a line 20' from the wall. From back to the wall position run to the first ball, pick up and throw as quickly as possible over the 8' mark, at the target. Return to the wall and repeat as many times as possible in the minute. Record the number of correct throws that hit the target.

7) Batting – Lofted Drive

Chalk or fix a large circular "bulls eye" on a wall at least 10' high if possible. Mark a batting crease approximately 20' away and facing the target. Bouncing a tennis ball at will try to hit the target with a lofted straight drive. Repeat, always commencing from a good stance position at the crease. Record the number of strokes made in one minute. (The straighter and harder the hit the quicker the ball will return.)

8) Bowling – Action

From the "coil" position bowl a tennis ball from a line 10 yds away from the wall, as hard as possible to bounce over a line marked 4' from the floor on the wall. Collect the ball as quickly as possible. Record the number of correct deliveries made in one minute.

9) Wicket-keeping or Slip Catching

Set a string or chalk line on a wall just high enough to touch with the outstretched fingers from a squat jump. From the wicket-keeper's squatting position jump and touch the line as many times as possible in one minute. Record the number of successes.

With a little initiative this type of cricket circuit can easily be adapted for pairs or small groups. For example, with Item 1 close catching can be done in pairs. With Item 3 bowlers can bowl to each other.

In all specific training care must be taken to ensure that the cricket skill is performed correctly. Bad habits can easily be developed and it is recommended that a good coach be on hand whenever possible.

7 Practice

Attitudes

Probably because it has never been properly defined, cricket practice, in terms of improving performance, has developed in a most illogical way over the years. Many cricketers seem to consider practice not as a means of improving their technique, but more as a light physical work-out. Indeed, I rather suspect that the average practice session does more harm than good to the majority of players. In many instances, it has developed into a social habit; a forerunner to the evening's entertainment! Not that I am saying that this cannot be an enjoyable and worthwhile part of cricketing life; it is, but let us recognise it as that. In fact, following discussions with many keen cricketers, I am very conscious of widening interest in cricket practice with a definite objective. I am therefore pleased to be able to present a few ideas, some of which are already bearing fruit, on what might be more realistic methods for improving technique.

Firstly, I must identify what we will be trying to achieve through making a few comparisons. In the normal net practice, any number of different types of bowler may bowl to a batsman for a given period of time, at the end of which there is a general change round and another batsman follows the same routine. In the well-organised practice, with a coach in charge, it is, of course, not so haphazard as I have suggested and there is no doubt that the coach can impart good advice to the players. However, it is one thing listening to advice, but another putting it into practice, especially if the chances of putting the advice into practice are, to say the least,

spasmodic. For example, a coach may notice a fault in a batsman when he is trying to drive an off-spinning half volley pitching on middle stump. The coach highlights the fault, shows the batsman how to play the stroke in question, but unfortunately the off-spinner happens to be one of five net bowlers and in the rest of the batsman's quarter of an hour in the net, of the half dozen or less deliveries bowled by the off-spinner, only one is a half volley pitching on middle stump or thereabouts! Need I say more?

Another example – in a recent match, the game was lost when the wicket-keeper twice missed stumping the batting team's star batsman in the last over. The bowler in question was a left-arm spin bowler with an unusual spinning action. It was only his second game in the first team. Unfortunately, in the net practice, it was found that there was no room for a wicket-keeper to stand behind the wicket in the net to practise taking the spin bowler. In addition, if it had been possible, the pitch was not very good and bowling with the left-arm spinner was the club's fast opening bowler to whom the wicket-keeper would always stand back anyway. Better luck next week!

Another example – again in a recent match, a young fast bowler of whom so much was expected really had a bad time. Not so much in that the batsmen found him easy to score off, but simply because he could not get through his run-up properly. He bowled ten no balls at least. This was not really surprising because he had been doing just that in the previous week's net practice. That is when he could actually get his full run-up in without another bowler getting in his way. On top of this, the young man had bowled for far too long.

Final example – bad coaching – in a quarter of an hour's net practice, a young batsman was corrected on six different strokes in four different positions on each stroke! Might it not have been better for the coach to have concentrated on one fault in maybe two strokes?

CONCLUSIONS

In my experience at all levels of the game, realistic, properly defined practice offers the best chance for keen cricketers to improve quickly. Haphazard nets, offering little effective practice, are a sure way of undermining inherent skill and certainly will not assist in the developing of new skills. The examples previously noted are just a few of the situations that prevail in the normal net practice. What is the answer? I submit that the whole subject of practice should be reviewed in depth by coaches and cricketers. The message that comes through from everyone is that a much greater emphasis must be put on specific training and practice.

Specific Practice (Fig 89)

Specific practice means training with a single objective in mind. In so far as cricket is concerned, this means trying to maximise the amount of practice of one skill that can be obtained in a given time. The preceding examples highlight the need to be objective if training is to be worthwhile. In batting, to practise a particular stroke, it is necessary for the ball to pitch within a few inches of a particular spot. If it doesn't, the stroke intended cannot be practised – it is as simple as that. It is quite logical, therefore, to ensure that in batting, a weak stroke is practised by dropping, throwing or bowling the ball accurately on to a point on the pitch that will allow the stroke to be played. For convenience, we can create the situation either by using a soft ball on a firm surface possibly indoors, or alternatively by using a cricket ball within the protection of a suitably designed cricket net. Both situations will give considerably more opportunity for the single skill to be practised than would be the case in a normal net practice, where a batsman may not receive one ball to which he could play the stroke he had hoped to practise. In this type of specific practice, whilst it is necessary for the ball to be delivered very accurately, care must be taken not to get too close to the batsman when serving the ball, hence the reason for the net to be suitably designed. A good bowling machine is ideal for specific batting practice. Batsmen should not play the stroke concerned unless they feel the ball has pitched correctly.

Specific practice of bowling is that much easier to control than batting, for obvious reasons. However, it still needs the consideration of sound planning, which means allowing the bowler concerned the freedom of being able to run up and deliver the ball without impedance from others in the bowling area. The same principles apply to fielding and wicket-keeping.

Whether the coach or the cricketer himself makes a conscious effort to improve technique through specific practice, there are still certain requirements without which specific practice will fail to realise its full potential. It may appear to be unnecessarily "fussy", but the very first requirement is to establish a form of recording of progress.

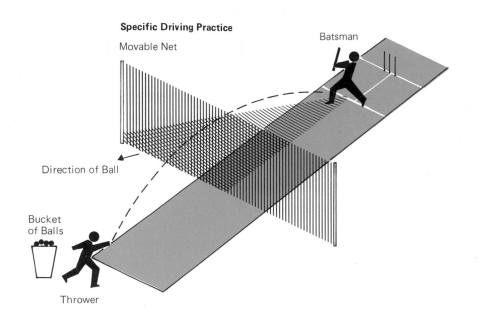

Specific Driving Practice

Movable Net

Batsman

Direction of Ball

Bucket
of Balls

Thrower

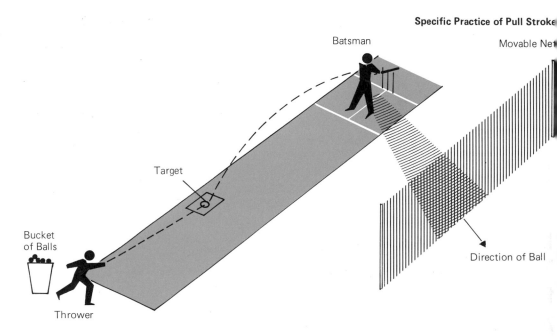

Specific Practice of Pull Stroke

Batsman

Movable Net

Target

Bucket
of Balls

Direction of Ball

Thrower

Fig. 89

The memory is not good enough and I am afraid that whilst it may go against the grain for a practical cricketer, the notebook and pencil are as good as anything, with the exception of the video tape recording, which is by far the best form of recording. If you are not conversant with the possibilities of video, take the time to investigate – it will be time well spent.

The first thing to be recorded is an assessment of individual ability as it stands, whether it be for a single skill or the whole range. This means recording strengths in addition to weaknesses. This is not a five minute job, and time should be taken to make a comprehensive assessment. Weaknesses should then be fully analysed and a policy should be established for, or by the individual player. Having established a policy, a programme of training and practice can be compiled and put into operation. At the end of the programme it will be possible to assess its value and look towards further improvements. A word of warning. Do not try too much in the first programme. Look to achieving a small, but definite improvement. A good coach will be a tremendous help to you in achieving your aims, but if a coach is not available, the whole operation can still go ahead with a colleague of similar enthusiasm. The following are examples of specific training and practice in batting and bowling:

Examples of Specific Training and Practice for Batting

ASSESSMENT NOTES

These can take a very simple form for the individual working with a colleague, or a more sophisticated record form can be designed if working in a group scheme. Personal details should be recorded (age, height, weight etc.), as should the detailed cricket background (record in regular teams etc.). An important section of the notes will be the details of the assessment and the period over which it is considered.

Assessment Period:
Three twenty minute normal net practice sessions (batting).
Dates:
....
Three innings played for the regular team, minimum total batting time, one hour.
Dates/Matches:
....

EXAMPLE ASSESSMENT (by coach in this instance)

1. Slow footwork.
2. General tendency to play forward too much.
3. No driving power on the off-side considering height and build.
4. Shows no inclination to play horizontal bat strokes off the back foot, probably due to the early forward movement.
5. Grip – top hand too far behind bat handle.
6. Stance – head too far over the off-side and stance too open.
7. Backlift – cramped left (front) arm bending too much, too early.
8. Initial forward movement – incorrect and too early. Someone has obviously told him to put his foot to the ball without mentioning head and shoulder as being more important.
9. Initial back movement. On the odd occasion he played back, he opened the body to face the bowler.

The Skills of Cricket

This young man can show almost immediate improvement by a little concentrated effort on three aspects of batting:

1. Fitness.
2. Correction of basics through grooving corrected stroke pattern in concentrated practice periods.
3. Developing confidence to hit the ball hard.

SUGGESTED PROGRAMME (Six Weeks)

Fitness
Six 30 minute individual circuit training sessions per week for six weeks.

Skills
a) Five half-hour specific practice sessions per week for first two weeks. Off-driving practice only with tennis ball or similar. Two participants only — batsman and thrower (plus machine if available). Check basics periodically. In these sessions practise both check and full follow-through drives.
b) For second two weeks repeat a), but using cricket balls.
c) Final two weeks — five half-hour net practises per week with two selected bowlers, both of whom will be trying to bowl half volleys on or outside the off-stump. The batsman should only play one attacking stroke — the off-drive. Otherwise defend, either forward or back. In the last session record possible dismissals.

The last five net sessions must take place on good pitches, either indoors or outdoors. The emphasis must be on driving the ball with full power. In the group type sessions (first four weeks) when the ball is positioned by throwing or bowling machine, intersperse the normal two-handed backlift by a top handed only backlift.

It is important that a final assessment is undertaken at the end of the programme. In all programmes of training, whether they be self-motivated or group organised, always think in terms of specific practice. If, for example, a bowling machine is available, use it to its best advantage, providing it does the job that you expect from it. At the same time, it should be realised that specific practice does not mean selfish practice. When assisting a colleague, it simply means that the assistant is taking his turn to provide the maximum realistic practice conditions possible.

Examples of Specific Training and Practice for Bowling
ASSESSMENT NOTES

General assessment details are as for batting, depending upon whether monitoring is by group or individual, for example:

Assessment Period:
  Two normal net sessions of one hour each.
Dates:
  ....
Three regular club matches; minimum number of thirty overs to be bowled.
Dates/Matches:
  ....

EXAMPLE ASSESSMENT

Both net sessions were video recorded. Matches were recorded by tape recorder and notebook. It was noticeable in both cases that as the bowler tired, direction suffered, rather than length. Over thirty per cent of deliveries pitched on and outside the leg-stump in the second half of both matches and practice sessions. Run-up is inconsistent, on occasions losing rhythm, possibly through a shortened stride approaching delivery. The bowler's quite lively pace comes from a fast arm action at delivery. His action at the wicket is quite good, but strained through his poor run-up. He does not seem to have any bowling plan and it is difficult to see what type of delivery he is trying to bowl.

SUMMARY AND SUGGESTED PROGRAMME (six weeks)

This young man has quite good potential. He is obviously not as fit as he should be for fast bowling and this, together with a poor run-up, causes the rapid deterioration in performance after only a few overs. Neither is there any sign of the concentration necessary in planning his bowling.

PROGRAMME

Three half-hour physical training sessions per week for all six weeks. A new training programme should be embarked upon at the beginning of next year, leading him into the season fully fit for real progress as a fast bowler. In conjunction with, or separate to the weekly physical training sessions, effort should be made to go through the following minimum programme of technique improvement:

First Three Weeks

Five half-hour net sessions per week (no batsman).

First fifteen minutes should be concentrated on developing new run-up. The new run-up should be established in consultation with a good coach, if possible. If not, follow good written advice on the subject. Short strides to long strides with acceleration and rhythm should be the theme. Study leading international bowlers. The remaining fifteen minutes should be concentrated on hitting a set target (1' wide × 2') positioned on a suitable length just outside the off-stump (using the new style run-up). Continually check basic action and look to develop swing bowling technique.

Second Three Weeks

Five one hour net sessions with batsman. Practice should not be with more than one other bowler and even then, the two bowlers should bowl six balls each consecutively (one over) as in a match. This will allow the over to be planned. Video record, if possible, but in any case, thoroughly analyse the whole practice.

GENERAL SUMMARY

The methods described can be adapted and improved upon with experience. Fielding and wicket-keeping practice can be accommodated into specific practice. Take care not to let specific training and practice dominate to the exclusion of other forms of practice and the playing of cricket games for fun and practice. In fact, specific practice can be integrated into some of the excellent cricket games that are now part of the cricket scene. The National Cricket Association's Proficiency Award Scheme Tests are also excellent training in the skills

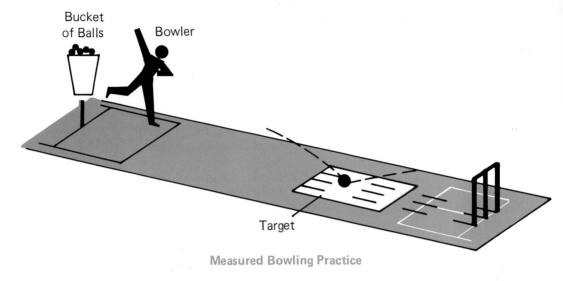

Bucket of Balls

Bowler

Target

Measured Bowling Practice

Fig. 90

of cricket for eight to eighteen year olds and provide much fun in addition to giving a sound measure of improvement in technique. Always try to make practice interesting. Divide your practice time to allow variation in activity and always commence with a warm-up session.

Measured Cricket Practice *(Fig 90)*

Based on the principles of Group Coaching and Circuit Training, I have found this method of practising to be very effective, as it simulates the combinations of requirements needed for improving skills. For example, it:

1. Gives skill practice in a variety of environments in or out of doors, obviating the need for a special cricket facility.
2. Measures skill improvement by setting achievable targets.
3. Improves physical fitness.
4. Improves concentration.

All the skills of cricket can be simulated by

setting up the required situation for the performing of the particular skill. It is important to define exactly what skill is to be practised and care should be taken that markers and floor markings are re-positioned exactly when the practice of the skill is repeated. A record of performance should be made during each practice session, i.e. number of balls hit between the markers, number of deliveries hitting the target area when bowling, etc. A challenge is then set and improvement, if any, can be gauged. Take particular note of any variations in pattern of performance over a long practice session, i.e. in the first two overs of a ten over bowling spot. It is a good idea for young players to keep a book recording their performances in all forms of training. Comparison may be made between this type of practice and the cricket circuit suggested in the Fitness chapter. Remember that there is a vital difference. In this instance, correct technique and success in directing the ball is the criterion. In the cricket circuit, speed of correct performance is the criterion, time being the measured

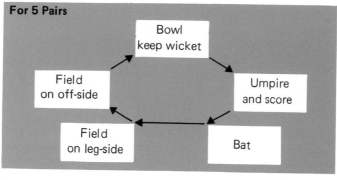

For 5 Pairs

Bowl keep wicket

Field on off-side

Umpire and score

Field on leg-side

Bat

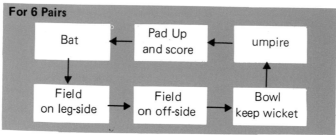

For 6 Pairs

Bat

Pad Up and score

umpire

Field on leg-side

Field on off-side

Bowl keep wicket

Rotation Examples for Pairs Cricket

Fig. 91

ingredient. When laying out the practice area and setting markers, take care to make the size and distance apart of the markers commensurate with ability. Always set an achievable goal, if not an easy one.

Cricket Games for Practice

Pairs and Eight-a-Side Cricket are marvellous cricket innovations giving enjoyable practice, as well as competition to players of all ages. They are games that are used too infrequently in the development of the game and its skills. Their greatest function is that they provide action for everyone. They are games that can be played in or out of doors, in sports halls or on cricket grounds, and they can be enjoyed using a soft or a hard ball.

PAIRS CRICKET *(Fig 91)*

The game is played in competition between pairs. In practice it can be designed to give practice to pairs of players in any of the game's skills. In a practice session for example, twelve players could follow the playing sequence to cover the time available. Any combination of pairs could be arranged. For example, if a form of specific practice was required, six batsmen could form three pairs and six bowlers could form three pairs, each pair rotating after an agreed number of overs.

In general, the rules of cricket would apply. Each pair bat for an agreed number of overs, regardless of whether they are dismissed or not. If a batsman is dismissed, an agreed number of runs is deducted from his score, which commences with a total of one hundred.

The deductable total can be set for any occasion, although eight has been found suitable for players under fourteen years of age and ten, twelve or more for older players. In a practice session, scores need not be kept, although it is recommended that they should be to add the element of

The Skills of Cricket

match play so necessary in practice.

EIGHT-A-SIDE CRICKET

As good as anything for both team practice and competition, Eight-a-Side Cricket is an extension of pairs cricket. Eight players (four pairs) form a team, each pair batting for an agreed number of overs. The team score commences with a total of two hundred. There is no need for individual scores to be kept; simply deduct an agreed number from the team total when a wicket falls. In its simplest form of practice, scores can be called after every score or wicket, by the umpire.

As can be imagined, there is a much greater accent on fielding in this game, as compared to eleven-a-side cricket, and as such, improvement in ground fielding can be spectacular.

RULES

The Laws of Cricket shall apply with the following exceptions:

1. Each team shall comprise eight players.
2. Each game shall consist of one innings per team, each innings to be of sixteen overs duration (twenty overs when time permits, or twelve overs when time is limited).
3. The batting side shall be divided into pairs, each pair batting for four overs and changing at the end of the fourth, eighth and twelfth over. In a twenty over game, at the end of the fifth, tenth and fifteenth over. In a twelve over game, at the end of the third, sixth and ninth over.
4. Batsmen shall have unlimited "lives", but each life shall result in eight runs (this may be varied, depending on the age group) being deducted from the total. Batsmen shall change ends at the fall of each wicket,

except on the last ball of an over.
5. Each player on the fielding side *must* bowl, with the exception of the wicket-keeper. No player shall bowl more than three overs (four overs in a twenty over game).
6. Each team shall commence its innings with a score of 200 runs.
7. The winning team shall be the side scoring the higher number of runs after deductions for the fall of wickets.
8. In all matches no fielder, except the wicket-keeper, shall be allowed to field nearer than eleven yards, measured from the middle stump, except behind the wicket on the off-side.

DURATION OF GAMES

Pairs and Eight-a-Side Cricket Games can be played within various limited periods of time. When arranging a match, organisers should emphasise the importance of not wasting time in changing over etc., i.e. a sixteen over match can be completed easily within two hours; twelve overs within one and a half hours, etc. I can see this game taking place at the highest level. Imagine spectators having the opportunity of seeing sixteen Test players displaying their skills – all within two or three hours.

CONTINUOUS CRICKET
(Fig 92)

This is a fun game that can be ideal for finishing off a practice or training session when time is too short to organise a pairs game. Whilst it is purely a fun game and has little to offer batsmen or bowlers in serious practice, there is ample scope to develop sound fielding techniques, providing there are not too many players.

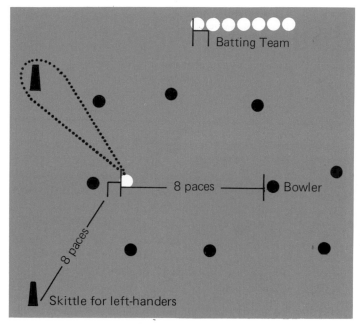

Layout for Continuous Cricket

Fig. 92

RULES

1. Number of complete innings per team should be decided before commencement of the game.

2. The ball must be delivered underhand to bounce no more than once before the wicket.

3. The bowler may bowl, whether or not a batsman is at the wicket.

4. The batsman must run every time he hits the ball.

5. To score a run, the batsman must run round the skittle and be in position to play a stroke at the next ball delivered.

6. A batsman can be "out" bowled, or caught only.

7. The umpire must call "out" immediately the batsman is dismissed.

8. The incoming batsman must remain seated on the batting chair until the previous batsman is given "out".

9. The umpire must call "No Ball" if the ball bounces more than once before reaching the wicket, or if the bowler delivers the ball in front of the bowling mark.

NOTE

Fielders should not be allowed nearer to the batsman than eight paces.

8 Equipment

Something I have noticed about the most successful players and teams is the way they are turned out. Looking the part is half-way towards playing the part and time and time again this adage is proved in matches. Nothing gives a team more of a "boost" than to find they are playing against a team who obviously do not care about their appearance. Successful players have pride and whether it be in performance or appearance, it should naturally become an integral part of any young player's development. Looking the part does not mean that every item of equipment must be the most expensive there is; it only means that it should be clean and well serviced. Young cricketers are very often persuaded to invest their hard earned savings in cheap equipment that looks well on the outside, but is shoddy on the inside. Take great care when selecting equipment. List the priorities and make sure that once equipment has been purchased, you also have the back-up materials to service it properly.

Bats and footwear are particularly important. Nothing would be more annoying than breaking a favourite bat through lack of care, and how foolish you would feel if you were run out by yards as a result of a missing spike! Before selecting equipment I strongly advise cricketers to contact a retailer who has a reputation for good service. Young players should ask senior players or coaches to recommend someone. Hard experience tells me that bargains are few and far between and most people get what they pay for.

BATS

There is no doubt that the majority of cricketers use too heavy a bat. I blame (with tongue in cheek) players like Viv Richards and Clive Lloyd who play with bats that most of us could not lift, let alone hit the ball with. A reasonable test for the weight of a bat is that it should be such that a batsman can easily manage a high and correct backlift using the top hand only (i.e. left hand for a right-handed batsman). Size is also an important consideration as is the length of the handle. I would never recommend the use of a long handle without a very careful assessment. Control of the bat is everything in good batsmanship and yet in general it is not given anything like the consideration it warrants.

Bats should be cared for by regular cleaning, using fine sandpaper as necessary and a light smear of bat or linseed oil as a preservative. Avoid oiling the splice, but oil the back of the bat when new as a seal against moisture. Repair edge cracks with a good quality glue and cover with adhesive tape. Make certain the grip is firm and in good condition — this is an essential. Break a bat in by bouncing a good quality leather ball on the hitting area until it has lost its initial softness and acquired a firm but resilient surface.

Unless one is in the millionaire class, be realistic in purchasing a bat. If playing regularly on bad wickets and having to hit cheap, two, or even one-piece "hard" balls, why go to the expense of buying the highest quality "soft" bat — which these days can be

Equipment

extremely expensive. There are excellent bats around made especially for the harder conditions that many clubs and school players have to endure. Do not scoff at a vellum covered bat; providing they are not too heavy they can give excellent service. If, however, it is a special occasion and a favourite relation insists on buying the bat, take time and select the bat with "feel" and balance. I was once advised by a fine Australian batsman, Jock Livingston, that an open grain (six to eight grains) gives the best performance, whilst a close grain bat wears the best — but willow is a natural product and hard and fast rules cannot be made. Jock, an expert in the trade, suggests that one should think of selecting a bat just as you would a pair of shoes.

PROTECTIVE EQUIPMENT

When talking of protective equipment I am always reminded of that great character and cricketer, Brian Close. I well remember the doubtful pleasure of watching him face a fearsome West Indian pace attack at Old Trafford in the late '70's. On a number of occasions he unnecessarily let fast short-pitched deliveries hit him in the chest and ribs, taking great care not to rub the spot that was obviously causing him great pain. I admired his bravery, but it certainly could not have had the effect of convincing the batsmen due to follow him that the bowling was easy. It is important to wear the protection necessary for the conditions if you are to acquire the confidence necessary to play the game.

Firstly, every cricketer should wear an athletic support with a pocket that will contain a protector or "box" as we call it. I see no reason why fielders in close catching positions or on bumpy out-fields should not be so equipped. In many instances they are

more likely to be hit than a batsman or wicket-keeper. A thigh pad may also be worn by batsmen to save unnecessary bruising.

The item of protective equipment that causes most discussion is the helmet, and whether or not it should be worn on all occasions. I think it is a matter for the individual, but youngsters may be guided by their mentors. Expense is a factor as helmets are very expensive. If they are available and there is obvious risk, I would advocate their use, especially when they may give that vital spark of confidence to a young player. I am not sure that I agree with their use in the field however, as I believe that those in charge of the game should not allow youngsters to field in ridiculous "suicide" positions. One of these days a young cricketer is going to be seriously hurt, whether he is wearing a helmet or not, and then maybe stronger action will be taken.

Pads, of course, are our next line of defence against physical hurt. There are many designs. Make sure to select light pads and, if necessary, cut off the loose ends of the leather straps.

Batting gloves are a necessity and care must be taken in their selection, mainly to make certain that they are comfortable and allow complete control of the bat — which very often they do not. Avoid tight-fitting clothing — nothing can put you off your game more. If anything, selecting a size too big can be a bonus, especially after a cleaning or a wash. I can hardly classify caps and sweaters under the heading "Protective Equipment", although I have known a cap save a nasty bump or two and it can protect the eyes against the glare of the sun. I have not made special mention of wicket-keeping gloves in this chapter, but have done so under the heading of "Wicket-keeping".

In the English climate sweaters are an

The Skills of Cricket

essential part of any cricketer's clothing. Under some circumstances a thick woollen sweater will protect you from more than the cold if you happen to be batting against a very fast bowler. An under-vest is also very useful in preventing stiffness and consequent injury after perspiring.

FOOTWEAR

There are so many different styles, selection of any one of them is difficult. Be sure that footwear is comfortable and allows for the wearing of thick woollen socks. Good quality footwear is a wise investment. Spiked boots are a must for most grounds and bowlers of any pace need to use them. Rubber soled footwear is only suitable for dry conditions, but an essential for indoor cricket.

Finally, remember to store your equipment properly, in clean conditions, particularly during the close season, and when the next match comes along you will have given yourself a better chance of enjoying the success your hard work has earned.

Appendix

Whilst this book is not intended to cover the Laws of Cricket, it is important that players thoroughly understand those laws that can influence their performance. In particular, the LBW and no ball laws should be studied, as they are vital in the development of technique. A knowledge of the laws will also give an appreciation of the umpire's job and perhaps persuade players that forgiveable mistakes can be made.

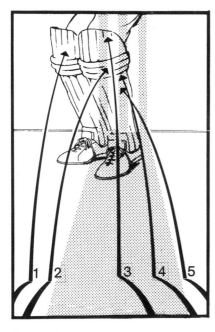

Leg before wicket

1 Not out.
2 Probably out but the umpire may rule not out if he feels the ball was turning sharply enough to have missed the stumps altogether.
3 Probably out but the umpire may rule not out if he feels the ball was still rising sharply.
4 Probably out but the umpire may rule not out if he feels the ball was turning so sharply that it would have missed off-stump.
5 Not out.

NOTE
If in 1. the ball was turning more, and in the umpire's opinion would have hit the stumps, the batsman could be given out if the batsman did not make a genuine attempt to play at the ball – even though the ball made contact with the batsman outside the line of the off-stump.

LAW 36   LEG BEFORE WICKET

Out LBW
The Striker shall be out LBW in the circumstances set out below:

(a) **Striker Attempting to Play the Ball**
The Striker shall be out LBW if he first intercepts with any part of his person, dress or equipment a fair ball which would have hit the wicket and which has not previously touched his bat or a hand holding the bat, provided that:

(i) The ball pitched, in a straight line between wicket and wicket or on the off side of the Striker's wicket, or in the case of a ball intercepted full pitch would have pitched in a straight line between wicket and wicket.
and
(ii) the point of impact is in a straight line between wicket and wicket, even if above the level of the bails.

(b) **Striker Making No Attempt to Play the Ball**
The Striker shall be out LBW even if the ball is intercepted outside the line of the off-stump, if, in the opinion of the Umpire, he has made no genuine attempt to play the ball with his bat, but has intercepted the ball with some part of his person and if the circumstances set out in (a) above apply.

131

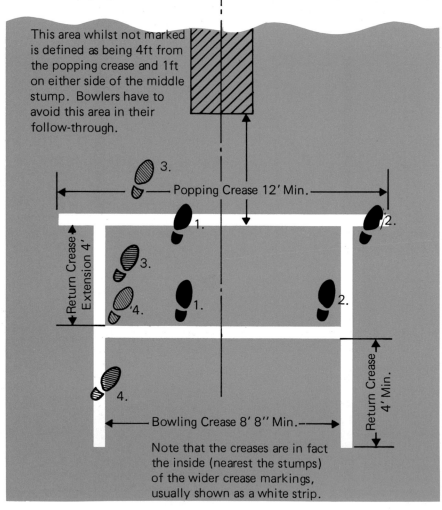

This area whilst not marked is defined as being 4ft from the popping crease and 1ft on either side of the middle stump. Bowlers have to avoid this area in their follow-through.

3.

Popping Crease 12' Min.

1.

2.

Return Crease Extension 4'

3.

4.

1.

2.

4.

Bowling Crease 8' 8" Min.

Return Crease 4' Min.

Note that the creases are in fact the inside (nearest the stumps) of the wider crease markings, usually shown as a white strip.

No Ball foot positions, important crease definitions and follow through restrictions

Positions 1 & 2 are Fair Deliveries
Positions 3 & 4 No Balls

Fig. 94

LAW 24   NO BALL

1. Mode of Delivery
The Umpire shall indicate to the Striker whether the Bowler intends to bowl over or round the wicket, overarm or underarm, or right or left-handed. Failure on the part of the Bowler to indicate in advance a change in his mode of delivery is unfair and the Umpire shall call and signal "no ball".

2. Fair Delivery – The Arm
For a delivery to be fair the ball must be bowled not thrown – see Note (a) below. If either Umpire is not entirely satisfied with the absolute fairness of a delivery in this respect he shall call and signal "no ball" instantly upon delivery.

3. Fair Delivery – The Feet
The Umpire at the bowler's wicket shall call and signal "no ball" if he is not satisfied that in the delivery stride:

(a) the Bowler's back foot has landed within and not touching the return crease or its forward extension

or

(b) some part of the front foot whether grounded or raised was behind the popping crease.

4. Bowler Throwing at Striker's Wicket Before Delivery
If the Bowler, before delivering the ball, throws it at the Striker's wicket in an attempt to run him out, the Umpire shall call and signal "no ball". See Law 42.12 (Batsman Unfairly Stealing a Run) and Law 38 (Run Out).

5. Bowler Attempting to Run Out Non-Striker Before Delivery
If the Bowler, before delivering the ball, attempts to run out the non-Striker, any runs which result shall be allowed and shall be scored as no balls. Such an attempt shall not count as a ball in the over. The Umpire shall not call "no ball". See Law 42.12 (Batsman Unfairly Stealing a Run).

6. Infringement of Laws by a Wicket-Keeper or a Fieldsman
The Umpire shall call and signal "no ball" in the event of the Wicket-Keeper infringing Law 40.1 (Position of Wicket-Keeper) or a Fieldsman infringing Law 41.2 (Limitation of On-side Fieldsmen) or Law 41.3 (Position of Fieldsmen).

7. Revoking a Call
An Umpire shall revoke the call "no ball" if the ball does not leave the Bowler's hand for any reason. See Law 23.2 (Either Umpire Shall Call and Signal "Dead Ball").

8. Penalty
A penalty of one run for a no ball shall be scored if no runs are made otherwise.

9. Runs From a No Ball
The Striker may hit a no ball and whatever runs result shall be added to his score. Runs made otherwise from a no ball shall be scored no balls.

10. Out From a No Ball
The Striker shall be out from a no ball if he breaks Law 34. (Hit the Ball Twice) and either Batsman may be Run Out or shall be given out if either breaks Law 33 (Handled the Ball) or Law 37 (Obstructing the Field).

11. Batsman Given Out Off a No Ball
Should a Batsman be given out off a no ball the penalty for bowling it shall stand unless runs are otherwise scored.

NOTES

(a) Definition of a Throw
A ball shall be deemed to have been thrown if, in the opinion of either Umpire, the process of straightening the bowling arm, whether it be partial or complete, takes place during that part of the delivery swing which directly precedes the ball leaving the hand. This definition shall not debar a Bowler from the use of the wrist in the delivery swing.

(b) No Ball not Counting in Over
A no ball shall not be reckoned as one of the over. See Law 22.3 (No Ball or Wide Ball).

Laws 24 and 36 have been printed by permission of the MCC. Copies of the current edition of the Laws of Cricket with full notes and interpretations can be obtained from the MCC at Lord's Cricket Ground, price 50p excluding postage.

Index